"I am a bread baker's granddaughter. Needless to say, Ali's familial connection to bread and all of its nostalgia hits close to home. In *Bread Toast Crumbs*, she makes the daunting feel doable: homemade bread can be no big deal! I love all of her inventive ideas for ways to use bread (her Crumbs section especially appeals to my can't-waste-a-thing heart). This book will be in heavy rotation in my house."

—JULIA TURSHEN

"I appreciate a cookbook that takes the fuss out of home bread baking—no overly complicated steps and skills required—just a straightforward recipe that yields something immeasurably better than store-bought. I'm excited about her Light Brioche recipe . . . brilliant! I will continue to turn back to these pages for both the variety of beautiful loaves and the suggestions of what to make to put on top of or between their slices. A real keeper."

—SARA FORTE

"Such a fun book that I kind of wish I had written it myself. Alexandra has combined creative and easy-to-make recipes with great know-how so anyone can make fantastic bread at home."

—JIM LAHEY

"After trying Alexandra's mom's once-secret peasant bread recipe, I never wanted to start another week without it. These are the lovable, crazy-simple, and un-mess-up-able loaves that will start a new home-baking revolution—and her brilliant recipes for using up every last crumb will sustain it."

—KRISTEN MIGLORE

"Does anything shout love and comfort louder than home-baked bread? Actually, yes—all of the recipes in this stunning collection do. Alexandra's recipes are sure to inspire yeast-o-phones and experts alike and her book is a wonderful reminder that breaking bread with people we love is literally one of the simplest and most meaningful things we can do for our families."

—JENNY ROSENSTRACH

"I'm a self-professed carb enthusiast, so Ali's beautiful book, *Bread Toast Crumbs*, speaks to my heart. Her approachable voice gives even the most novice of bakers (myself included) encouragement that they, too, can bake and bake beautifully. This book not only provides straightforward and inventive recipes for bread, but it also gets you thinking creatively about ways to incorporate it into every meal, in every way. Simply put, I love it."

—COLU HENRY

Bread Toast Crumbs

CLARKSON POTTER/PUBLISHERS
NEW YORK

BREAD TOAST CRUMBS

RECIPES FOR NO-KNEAD LOAVES AND MEALS TO SAVOR EVERY SLICE

—

ALEXANDRA STAFFORD

with Liza Lowery

Photographs by Eva Kolenko

To my mother

CONTENTS

For years, anytime somebody asked my mother for her peasant bread recipe, she credited King Arthur Flour, noting that it could be found on the back of the bread flour bag. This, of course, was a lie. My mother shared her recipe with nobody. The bread was the star of every dinner party she threw. No matter what magnificent dishes she served—whole roasted beef tenderloin, grilled cedar-planked salmon, clay-pot-braised lamb shoulder—her guests wanted to go home with one and only one recipe.

Growing up, I ate the bread at nearly every meal: toasted and sprinkled with cinnamon and sugar for breakfast; broiled with yellow mustard, raw onions, and Gruyère cheese for lunch; freshly baked and spread with butter alongside dinner.

When I moved away from home, what I missed most was my mother's bread, and I soon began making it regularly. I made it for my roommates in college and, when I moved to Philadelphia, for my classmates in cooking school. I made it for family meals when I worked in restaurants, and later for my friends at the newspaper where I worked as the food editor before starting my blog, *Alexandra's Kitchen*. Despite being surrounded by artisan bakeries at every turn, I never stopped making my mother's bread—it had become my party trick, too.

I didn't dare share the recipe—I was under strict orders not to. On the blog, I wrote about the local markets, restaurants, and farms, and the fun things I had learned while working in kitchens: tempura squash blossoms stuffed with herbed ricotta, pan-seared duck confit, and the like. But as the years went on (and my gaggle of children began amassing), I started sharing more family recipes, focusing on the food I had grown up on—honey-soy chicken wings from *The New York Times Cookbook*, butter-milk blueberry breakfast cake, Greek salad with my aunt Phyllis's dressing. It was the food I found myself craving once again. The bread was part of that.

Every so often I would sneak a photo of it into a blog entry—on a grilled cheese sandwich or beside a salad—and inevitably a reader would ask, "May I have your mother's bread recipe?" I answered as I had been taught and directed people to the back of the flour bag. But leading them astray—keeping this knowledge from so many people—grew tiresome. When one person noted there wasn't even a recipe on the bag, I knew it was time to revise my story. I needed permission to share the recipe.

I called my mom one day and pleaded. People all over the Internet fear yeast! The bread failures are rampant! No one knows how *easy* it can be! My mother finally acquiesced, and I hit publish on the post I'd drafted for weeks. I suspected the reception would be good, but I didn't quite anticipate *how* good. Before long, the comments poured in. The recipe inspired many who had deemed bread baking an impossibility to give it a try, and their resulting loaves exceeded expectations.

It's the simplicity that is the real beauty of this peasant bread. The no-knead dough comes together in under five minutes, rises in about one hour, and after a second short rise, bakes in buttered bowls. There's no trick to turn your oven into a professional oven. No trick to trap the steam to create bronzed crackling crusts, rustic scored surfaces. No trick to make the bread appear artisan. Peasant bread, with its blond, buttery crust, is the antithesis of artisan.

But the process is still rewarding: watching dough grow and transform, filling a house with comforting smells, savoring something so delectable made from such basic ingredients. Few kitchen endeavors produce such a sense of achievement—of triumph—as making bread, and nothing, it seems, elicits more gratitude for such little effort.

And yet many people, seasoned cooks included, fear the process and would sooner crank out sheets of pasta dough or deep-fry a turkey than open a packet of yeast. Despite the efforts of baking luminaries who have enlightened home cooks with simple tricks, bread hasn't been able to shake its high-maintenance reputation. But good bread— *really* good bread—can be made simply and quickly. Loaves that can feed a family for the week can be made in less than three hours. *Boules* to accompany a nice meal need not be started a day in advance. Good bread can be made without a starter, without a slow or cold fermentation, without an understanding of bakers' percentages, without being fluent in the baking vernacular: hydration, fermentation, biga, poolish, soaker, autolyse, barm. (None of these words, by the way, will appear in the recipes that follow.)

In the years since I published my mother's recipe on my blog, millions of people have visited the post, and many have credited it with giving them the confidence to get bread on the table any day of the week. And that's what I hope this book will do foremost: encourage anyone—the beginner baker, the busy professional, the time-strapped parent—to start making bread. And if it acts as a portal to more ambitious bread-making endeavors, I hope these bread bakers appreciate this recipe even more and return to it because they know peasant bread—soft crumbed, golden crusted— truly is as delicious as the rest.

But this book isn't just about baking bread and eating it: it's about what to do with those bags or bins filled with heels and nubs from your many loaves. Because, as you will soon discover—lucky you!—with a stash of day-old bread in the freezer, a world beyond crostini awaits, and there is nothing stale about it: soft-boiled eggs meet vinaigrette-bathed toasts, *pangrattato* showers orecchiette with brown butter and Brussels sprouts, French toast becomes savory with thyme and Parmesan, and bread-crumb chimichurri dresses rack of lamb. From sandwich to salad to soup to sauce, bread will continue to surprise you with its resilience and adaptability.

LOAF TO CRUMB

IT'S HARD NOT TO WAX POETIC ABOUT THE BREAD-BAKING PROCESS—THE TIME, THE GROWTH, THE SMELLS, THE AWE IT INSPIRES. BUT THE REASONS TO BAKE BREAD ASIDE FROM ROMANCE ARE SIMPLE: FOREMOST, FLAVOR—HOMEMADE BREAD TASTES BETTER THAN ANYTHING YOU CAN FIND AT THE STORE. SECOND, HEALTH—YOU KNOW EXACTLY WHAT'S IN YOUR HOMEMADE BREAD. THIRD, COST—A HOMEMADE LOAF OF BREAD REQUIRES ABOUT A DOLLAR'S WORTH OF PANTRY ITEMS. AND FOURTH, EASE—THERE'S REALLY NOTHING TO IT.

The first recipe in this book gives you each step of the process detailed and demystified. It will produce two golden loaves, fit for serving for dinner or toasting for breakfast. Most important, it will leave you with the confidence to tackle anything in the first part of this book, BREAD: various *boules,* buns, pullman loaves, pull-apart breads, pizza, focaccia, and dinner rolls. Each is an adaptation of the master recipe.

Many of these breads can (and should!) be used for the recipes in the TOAST and CRUMBS sections, but you do not need to bake your own bread to have success with those recipes. They will find new and delicious purpose for any heel, slice, or loaf aging in your kitchen. In Toast, fresh slices of bread are first used in sandwiches, flanking the likes of tarragon chicken salad (see page 121) and crabmeat with sauce *gribiche* (see page 123). As the bread ages, the slices meet the broiler (see page 151), the grill grates (see page 114), the sauté pan (see page 132), and finally the custard bath (see page 142).

In Crumbs, bread is broken down further. In addition to highlighting some classic day-old bread revivals—panzanella salad (see page 169),

bread pudding (see page 236)—this part explores bread's workhorse capabilities: as a thickener for soups and sauces, as a *panade*, or bread soaked in liquid, in meatballs (see page 229) and meat loaves (see page 232), and as a medium for transforming modest ingredients into hearty fare. These uses perhaps best illustrate bread's resilience and reflect how bread has been used loaf-to-crumb for centuries. And this is the real beauty of bread: its ability to endure, to become something else, and to nourish at every phase of its existence.

Each of these three parts—Bread, Toast, and Crumbs—is divided into subsections: Bread into *Savory Boules, Freeform Breads,* and *Sweet Breads;* Toast into *Salads, Soups, and Starters, Sandwiches, Entrées,* and *Sweets;* Crumbs into *Salads, Soups, and Starters, On the Side, Pasta, Meatless Mains, Meat and Fish,* and *Sweets.* To easily navigate through each part, just look for the text along the bottom of each page, where you will find the subsection referenced.

The recipes in this book, inspired by family, friends, my time working in restaurant kitchens, meals out, and my favorite cookbooks, celebrate bread in its entirety. Twenty years after baking my first loaf, I have found that the awe it inspires persists. Bread is what greets me in the morning, what sustains me throughout the day, and what I still look forward to most in the evening no matter the form: freshly baked, toasted, or crumbled all over my plate.

Let's take a look at what we need before we get started.

EQUIPMENT

Most of the recipes in this book require minimal equipment, which you likely have on hand, but here are the essentials:

- A large 4-quart bowl is ideal for mixing each recipe in the Bread section.

- Every baking book recommends measuring by weight, and for good reason: a digital scale foremost is more accurate than dry measuring cups. Depending on who is measuring, 1 cup of flour may weigh anywhere from 4 to 6 ounces. Multiply this by 4, and the final amount of flour for the Peasant Bread Master Recipe (page 22) will vary considerably, which will affect the taste and texture of the bread. A scale eliminates this human error.

  Using a scale is also faster than using measuring cups. Opening a bag of flour and dumping it into a bowl set on a tared scale takes far less time than scooping and leveling.

- 2- and 4-cup liquid measures

- A standard set of measuring spoons for measuring anything in small quantities (yeast, sugar, salt, spices)

- A standard set of dry measuring cups for nuts, herbs, cheese, and bread crumbs

- A wire whisk for blending dry ingredients

- A rubber spatula for mixing the dough

- A large tea towel, bowl cover (cloth or plastic), or plastic wrap for covering the bowl in which the dough is rising

- You will have the best results with most of the bread recipes in this book if you use two 1-quart Pyrex bowls, which are readily available and affordable in shops and online. The vintage 1.5-pint Pyrex 441 will produce a beautifully rounded *boule*, though locating one will require an eBay, flea market, or secondhand shop search. The more modern, plain glass versions work just fine.

  If you don't have two 1-quart bowls, you may use other vessels, though even slight differences in pan sizes dramatically affect the shape of the finished loaves. With 1.5-quart bowls, for example, the loaves will be wider and flatter. For better results when using 1.5-quart bowls, multiply the quantities in the ingredients lists by 1.5. The full recipe can be baked in one 2-quart bowl, but be sure to bake it for 10 minutes longer.

- For the loaf pan recipes, you will have the best results with two 8.5 × 4.5-inch loaf pans. A 9 × 5-inch loaf pan will create a shorter, wider loaf and will require a longer second rise. Many of the *boule* recipes that call for the 1-quart bowls can be adapted for the loaf pan by multiplying the quantities by 1.5.

- It's funny to see an oven listed as important equipment in a cookbook—it seems obvious. But for bread baking, you'll need a warm place for your dough to rise. Here's my favorite trick: set your oven to 400°F and let it preheat for one minute, then shut it off. The temperature will be between 80°F and 100°F. You should be able to place your hands on the oven grates without burning them. What's most important is that your dough rises in a warm, draft-free spot—it will really help the first rise happen in a timely manner.

FOR OTHER RECIPES, YOU'LL ALSO NEED:

- 13 × 18-inch rimmed sheet pan

- 12-cup muffin tin

- 8- or 9-inch cast-iron skillet or baking pan

- Bundt pan or Dutch oven
- A food processor is particularly handy for making crumbs as well as preparing nut butters, mincing herbs, and emulsifying dressings.
- A large silicone mat is especially useful for shaping hamburger buns, monkey breads, cinnamon-swirl bread, buttermilk pull-apart bread, etc.—any of the breads that requires shaping. King Arthur Flour sells a nice 18 × 24-inch mat that can be rolled up and tucked away, but these mats are readily available online and in cookware shops as well.
- A 9 × 13-inch baking pan
- A good 8-inch chef's knife
- A sharp 10-inch serrated knife for slicing bread

INGREDIENTS

Because bread baking requires so few ingredients, the quality of each is important, and subtle differences can have a great effect. Let's look at the ingredients used most often throughout the book in more detail.

FLOUR
Most of the bread recipes here call for unbleached all-purpose flour, which will yield a better-smelling and tastier loaf than bleached. Bleaching flour not only removes some of its protein but also imparts a metallic flavor, which can leave an unpleasant aftertaste. Unbleached all-purpose flour from King Arthur Flour, Hodgson Mill, Arrowhead Mills, and Bob's Red Mill are high quality and readily available. You can use bread flour, which is higher in protein than all-purpose flour, with equal success.

Whole-wheat flour, which is milled from the complete wheat kernel, will yield a denser loaf than all-purpose flour. When using whole-wheat flour, I prefer to use King Arthur Flour's white whole-wheat flour, which produces a lighter texture with a milder flavor than traditional whole-wheat flour. Graham flour and spelt flour, both of which are 100 percent whole wheat, can also be used when whole-wheat flour is called for.

There have been many breakthroughs with gluten-free baking, but gluten-free *bread* baking can still be challenging. Fortunately there are many high-quality gluten-free flour mixes on the market now that make it much easier. I find Cup4Cup, chef Thomas Keller's brand of gluten-free flour, produces a loaf that closely resembles the master loaf in texture. Or, feel free to use your favorite gluten-free mix or make your own (see page 56).

YEAST
Instant yeast, sometimes labeled as "rapid-rise," "fast-rising," or "bread machine yeast," is more concentrated than active dry yeast. It's easy to use because it doesn't have to be hydrated or "bloomed" with water first, which means it can be whisked directly in with the dry ingredients, making it as familiar an ingredient as baking soda or baking powder. Eliminating the blooming step also helps the process move along incredibly quickly.

SAF-Instant yeast, my preference, can be ordered in bulk from various online sources. Transfer it from its bag to a plastic quart container and store it in the fridge or freezer for months. Using yeast in bulk, moreover, gives you the flexibility of easily adjusting quantities without having to open a new packet, each of which typically contains 2¼ teaspoons, which is what most of the recipes that follow call for as well. Some of the bread recipes, particularly the ones that include whole-wheat flours, grains, nuts, and seeds, as well as the sweeter

loaves, benefit from an additional ¼ or ½ teaspoon of yeast to keep the texture light, as indicated.

But the best part about using instant yeast is this: it allows you to pack the dry ingredients (flour, salt, sugar, and instant yeast) in a zip-top bag and bring them with you wherever you travel. Pack your bowls and your peasant bread mix, and when you arrive at your destination, all you need is 2 cups of lukewarm water. People will think you are a genius.

WATER
Many of the bread recipes here call for lukewarm water. What does that mean? Use 1 part boiling water to 3 parts cold water. For most, this means ½ cup boiling water and 1½ cups cold water. This trick will create perfectly lukewarm water every time—no need to take its temperature. If water is not specified as lukewarm, that means room temperature will do just fine.

BUTTER
All the bread recipes call for butter for greasing. Butter, as opposed to other fats, creates not only a beautifully golden crust but also an incredibly tasty one. It is important to be generous with the butter when greasing, which means it must be softened to room temperature—cold butter will be hard to smear and thus less effective at creating a nonstick barrier between the bread and the bowl. To quickly soften butter, pop it in the microwave at 5-second intervals or grate it on a box grater, then set it near a warm spot for 5 minutes. For both greasing and baking, unsalted butter is preferable to salted to prevent the breads from tasting overly salty.

If you're looking for a vegan substitute, Earth Balance or vegan shortening (many shortenings are vegan, but check the label) works well. Nonstick cooking spray is good, too. A generous amount of coconut oil, not melted, will also work, though not as well.

NEUTRAL OIL
Whenever neutral oil is called for, use grapeseed, organic canola, or olive oil, all of which are mild in flavor and preferable to extra-virgin olive oil, whose strong flavor tends to dominate. My preference for both baking and cooking is grapeseed oil, which is nearly flavorless and has a high smoke point, allowing it to cook without smoking at high temperatures. Extra-virgin olive oil, while best for dressings and uncooked sauces, will taste bitter when heated for too long at high temperatures.

BREAD CRUMBS
Whenever *fresh* bread crumbs are called for, this simply means bread (day old is best, but fresh is fine, too) pulsed in the food processor. See the Note on page 172.

Whenever *dried* bread crumbs are called for, this means bread pulsed in the food processor, then dried in the oven (see page 178), or store-bought unseasoned dried bread crumbs, preferably panko, which are readily available everywhere.

SALT
When kosher salt is called for, use a brand like Diamond Crystal, which is coarser than most other brands.

When nice sea salt is called for, use something flaky like Maldon or fleur de sel.

One final tip before before you bust open that flour bag: take some time to organize your kitchen. With small jars of salt and sugar on the counter, yeast in a user-friendly container, a teapot on the stovetop, and a scale nearby, you're paving the way for bread baking to become a ritual, not a once-a-month event.

Now, let's get cooking!

THE PEASANT BREAD MASTER RECIPE

MAKES TWO 14-OUNCE LOAVES

Here it is. The no-knead bread recipe my mother has been making for forty years, the one she taught me to make twenty years ago, the recipe I published on my blog in 2012, the recipe that inspired the creation of every recipe that follows in this book.

This formula is simple—4 cups flour, 2 cups water, 2 teaspoons each salt and sugar, and 2¼ teaspoons yeast—and can be adapted in countless ways. Make it once as described below, then tailor it to your liking. Read Four Tips to Ensure Each Loaf Is a Success (page 27) before getting started, and read Variations (page 26) for hints on making changes.

4 cups (512 g) unbleached all-purpose flour

2 teaspoons kosher salt

2 teaspoons sugar

2¼ teaspoons instant yeast

2 cups lukewarm water (see page 20)

Softened unsalted butter, for greasing

1. In a large bowl, whisk together the flour, salt, sugar, and instant yeast. Add the water. Using a rubber spatula, mix until the water is absorbed and the ingredients form a sticky dough ball.

2. Cover the bowl with a damp tea towel or plastic wrap and set aside in a warm spot (see page 16) to rise for 1 to 1½ hours, until the dough has doubled in bulk.

3. Set a rack in the middle of the oven and preheat it to 425°F. Grease two 1-quart oven-safe bowls with the softened butter—be generous. Using two forks, deflate the dough by releasing it from the sides of the bowl and pulling it toward the center. Rotate the bowl quarter turns as you deflate, turning the mass into a rough ball.

4. Using your two forks and working from the center out, separate the dough into two equal pieces. Use the forks to lift each half of the dough into a prepared bowl. If the dough is too wet to transfer with forks, lightly grease your hands with butter or oil, then transfer each half to a bowl. Do not cover the bowls. Let the dough rise on the countertop near the oven (or another warm, draft-free spot) for 10 to 20 minutes, until the top of the dough just crowns the rims of the bowls.

5. Transfer the bowls to the oven and bake for 15 minutes. Reduce the heat to 375°F and bake for 17 to 20 minutes more, until evenly golden all around. Remove the bowls from the oven and turn the loaves out onto cooling racks. If the loaves look pale, return them to their bowls and bake for 5 minutes longer. Let the loaves cool for 15 minutes before cutting.

BREAD

The recipes here follow a simple no-knead mixing process: whisk together the dry ingredients, add the wet, mix with a spatula until combined. If you can make the Peasant Bread Master Recipe (page 22) (and you can!), you can also make all the others, as each, in essence, is an adaptation. In simple variations, nuts, seeds, cheese, herbs, and dried fruit enter the equation. In slightly more complex variations, grains (bulgur, oatmeal, cornmeal) are briefly soaked prior to mixing. In some cases, the liquid is infused with herbs or tea.

These recipes will also show how the dough can be adapted into other vessels (loaf pans, skillets, sheet pans, and muffin tins, to name a few) and applications (pizza, focaccia, and pull-apart breads). And just a handful of recipes deviates from the main assembly process, asking you to use your hands. Being liberal with the flour and letting the dough rest when directed will allow these breads to come together as seamlessly as the others, and the reward is well worth the extra effort: hamburger buns to bring to the barbecue all summer, cinnamon swirl bread for breakfast toast, buttermilk pull-apart rolls at the dinner table, pizza, egg-topped or crème fraîche–slicked, for any time of day, and so on.

VARIATIONS

The key to creating successful variations on the Peasant Bread Master Recipe is to stick to the basic ratio: 4 cups (512 g) of flour to 2 cups of liquid with (about) 2 teaspoons each of salt, sugar, and yeast. The proportions can vary slightly, and it's best to change one variable at a time, but if you keep this ratio in mind as you substitute flours and add seeds, nuts, herbs, spices, fruit, and cheeses, you are likely to create a tasty loaf every time.

As you add more nuts, seeds, and whole-grain flours—all of which make for a heavier loaf—you may need to increase the yeast to keep the texture of the bread light. Additionally, sugar and fat slow down the rising, so loaves with high amounts of sugar, oil, and/or butter benefit from a touch more yeast and longer rising periods.

Here are a few basic guidelines to follow as you invent your own variations on the master loaf:

- **OIL:** add as much as ¼ cup, such as olive, grapeseed, canola, walnut, or almond.

- **GRATED CHEESE:** add no more than 8 ounces.

- **FRESH HERBS:** start with a teaspoon or two.

- **DRIED HERBS:** start with ½ teaspoon.

- **SEEDS:** add as much as ½ cup; toasted seeds add more flavor.

- **NUTS:** add as much as 1½ cups; toasted nuts add more flavor.

- **DRIED FRUIT:** add as much as 1 cup, diced, if necessary.

- **FLOURS:** substitute 1 cup (about 128 g) at a time, gradually adding more to taste.

- **CORNMEAL:** add as much as ⅓ cup.

- **SWEETENERS:** omit the sugar or use others such as honey, maple syrup, molasses, or agave in the same proportion. When using ¼ cup or more of a liquid sweetener, you may have to compensate with more flour; when the amount is small (1 to 2 tablespoons), you shouldn't have to make any adjustments. Loaves with a higher sugar quantity will brown more quickly, so you should bake these sweeter loaves at 350°F or 375°F.

PRESERVING BREAD

If you know you're going to eat your homemade bread within a few days, store it at room temperature in a bread box, paper or cloth bag, or unsealed plastic bag—airtight plastic bags will keep your bread soft, but the bread will mold more quickly. Room-temperature storage is preferable, as refrigeration will actually dry out the bread faster.

If you have too much bread on hand to use within a few days, you can do several things to preserve it:

1. **FREEZE THE LOAVES.** Freezing the loaves whole or in large pieces gives you the most flexibility: if you need slices for French toast (see pages 140 and 151) or stratas (see pages 142 and 145), or if you need "big crumbs" for a panzanella salad (see page 169) or savory bread pudding (see page 210), simply thaw the loaf and proceed with the recipe. If you need "small crumbs" for a gratin (see pages 195, 203, 204, and 207), *pancotto* (see page 217), or a soup (see pages 180 and 182), thaw the loaf, break it up or whizz it in a food processor, and proceed with the recipe. If you eat a lot of toast, freeze bread in well-wrapped bundles of four or five slices; thaw at room temperature.

2. **FREEZE THE CRUMBS.** Having a stash of "fresh" bread crumbs (bread crumbs that haven't been oven dried) in the freezer is so handy. Because frozen crumbs thaw at room temperature in no time, any recipe that calls for fresh crumbs can materialize quite quickly. Store the fresh crumbs in the freezer in an airtight bag or container.

3. **MAKE DRIED BREAD CRUMBS.** If you often make cutlets or other breaded foods, it's especially nice to have on hand a vat of dried bread crumbs (see page 198), which taste superior to store-bought bread crumbs and will last nearly forever stored at room temperature in an airtight container.

Reheating a loaf or portion of a loaf on a pie plate or small sheet pan for 7 to 10 minutes at 375°F will restore its freshness. Toasting will do the same.

MAKE IT AHEAD

Any of the doughs here can be mixed ahead of baking. Simply follow the recipes as directed, but let the dough rise in the fridge instead of in a warm place. After 8 to 10 hours, the dough will be ready to be deflated, and you can proceed with the recipe. Just be aware that because the dough will be cold, the second rise may take as long as 1 to 2 hours.

To bring the dough to a party and bake it on the premises, simply mix it as directed and wrap the bowl tightly with plastic wrap. The dough can be deflated with forks as needed en route to or at the party before it is baked.

FOUR TIPS TO ENSURE EACH LOAF IS A SUCCESS

1. Use the right pans for the right job, and grease them well (see page 16).

2. Use instant yeast (see page 17).

3. Use a scale (see page 16).

4. Use lukewarm water (see page 20), and create a warm place for your bread to rise (see page 16).

THREE SEED BREAD

MAKES 2 LOAVES

Toasted seeds, a simple addition to any loaf of bread, go a long way in providing texture and weight and imparting a subtle nutty flavor. When freshly baked, this bread can be used for sandwiches, such as Crab Salad Sandwiches with Sauce Gribiche (see page 123). Day old, toast it and spread with salted butter, almond butter (see page 117), or jam.

¼ cup (40 g) sunflower seeds

¼ cup (40 g) pumpkin seeds

¼ cup (35 g) sesame seeds

4 cups (512 g) unbleached all-purpose flour

2 teaspoons kosher salt

2 teaspoons sugar

2¼ teaspoons instant yeast

2 cups lukewarm water

¼ cup neutral oil

Softened unsalted butter, for greasing

1. In a large skillet over medium heat, toast the sesame seeds until they are fragrant, lightly golden, and beginning to pop, 5 to 7 minutes. Transfer the seeds to a plate and let cool, about 10 minutes.

2. In a large bowl, whisk together the flour, salt, sugar, and instant yeast. Add the toasted seeds and whisk to combine. Add the water, followed by the oil. Using a rubber spatula, mix until the liquid is absorbed and the ingredients form a sticky dough ball. Cover the bowl with a damp tea towel or plastic wrap and set aside in a warm spot to rise for 1 to 1½ hours, until the dough has doubled in bulk.

3. Set a rack in the middle of the oven and preheat it to 425°F. Grease two 1-quart oven-safe bowls with the softened butter—be generous. Using two forks, deflate the dough by releasing it from the sides of the bowl and pulling it toward the center. Rotate the bowl quarter turns as you deflate, turning the mass into a rough ball.

4. Using your two forks and working from the center out, separate the dough into two equal pieces. Use the forks to lift each half of dough into a prepared bowl. If the dough is too wet to transfer with forks, lightly grease your hands with butter or oil, then transfer each half to a bowl. Do not cover the bowls. Let the dough rise on the countertop near the oven (or another warm, draft-free spot) for 10 to 20 minutes, until the top of the dough just crowns the rims of the bowls.

5. Transfer the bowls to the oven and bake for 15 minutes. Reduce the heat to 375°F and bake for 17 to 20 minutes more, until golden all around. Remove the bowls from the oven and turn the loaves out onto cooling racks. If the loaves look pale, return them to their bowls and bake for 5 minutes longer. Let the loaves cool for 15 minutes before cutting.

ROSEMARY SEMOLINA BREAD
WITH PINE NUTS

MAKES 2 LOAVES

Semolina flour, sometimes labeled as "pasta flour," is a yellow-hued, sandy-textured, high-gluten flour that lends a creamy texture to baked goods. Its subtle sweet and nutty flavor complements the earthy, musky notes of rosemary, which is why the two are often paired together in both sweet (cakes, cookies) and savory (pasta, bread) applications. Here, toasted pine nuts add texture to this golden-crumbed loaf, nice with Broiled Lamb Meatballs (see page 230), as the bread in Halloumi and Bread Skewers with Bagna Cauda (see page 173), in Greek Panzanella salad (see page 170), or beside any other dish with Mediterranean flavors.

½ cup (70 g) pine nuts

3½ cups (450 g) unbleached all-purpose flour

⅓ cup (66 g) fine semolina flour

2 teaspoons kosher salt

2 teaspoons sugar

2¼ teaspoons instant yeast

1 tablespoon finely chopped fresh rosemary

2 cups lukewarm water

¼ cup neutral oil

Softened unsalted butter, for greasing

1. In a large dry skillet, toast the pine nuts over medium-low heat, stirring, until they turn golden, 5 to 7 minutes. Transfer to a plate to cool, about 5 minutes.

2. In a large bowl, whisk together the flours, salt, sugar, instant yeast, and rosemary. Add the toasted nuts and toss to coat. Add the water, followed by the oil. Using a rubber spatula, mix until the liquid is absorbed and the ingredients form a sticky dough ball. Cover the bowl with a damp tea towel or plastic wrap and set aside in a warm spot to rise for 1 to 1½ hours, until the dough has doubled in bulk.

3. Set a rack in the middle of the oven and preheat it to 425°F. Grease two 1-quart oven-safe bowls with the softened butter—be generous. Using two forks, deflate the dough by releasing it from the sides of the bowl and pulling it toward the center. Rotate the bowl quarter turns as you deflate, turning the mass into a rough ball.

4. Using your two forks and working from the center out, separate the dough into two equal pieces. Use the forks to lift each half of dough into a prepared bowl. If the dough is too wet to transfer with forks, lightly grease your hands with butter or oil, then transfer each half to a bowl. Do not cover the bowls. Let the dough rise on the countertop near the oven (or another warm, draft-free spot) for 10 to 20 minutes, until the top of the dough just crowns the rims of the bowls.

5. Transfer the bowls to the oven and bake for 15 minutes. Reduce the heat to 375°F and bake for 17 to 20 minutes more, until golden all around. Remove the bowls from the oven and turn the loaves out onto cooling racks. If the loaves look pale, return them to their bowls and bake for 5 minutes longer. Let the loaves cool for 15 minutes before cutting.

QUINOA AND FLAX BREAD

MAKES 2 LOAVES

If adding uncooked quinoa to bread dough sounds like a mistake (or a recipe for unpleasantly crunchy bread) consider what quinoa is: a seed, and one that behaves like a grain when cooked, but that on its own—like flax, sesame, and poppy—adds flavor, texture, and visual appeal to baked goods. Here, red quinoa looks especially striking, though any variety will do. You can substitute millet for the quinoa and any other seed for the flax. Use this bread for the Tarragon Chicken Salad Sandwiches (page 121) or the Endive and Fava Salad Tartines with Herbed Ricotta (page 108), or simply slather it with butter for morning toast.

4 cups (512 g) unbleached all-purpose flour

2 teaspoons kosher salt

2 teaspoons sugar

2¼ teaspoons instant yeast

½ cup (100 g) red quinoa, rinsed

¼ cup (46 g) flaxseeds

2 cups lukewarm water

¼ cup neutral oil

Softened unsalted butter, for greasing

1. In a large bowl, whisk together the flour, salt, sugar, and instant yeast. Add quinoa and flaxseeds and toss to coat. Add the water, followed by the oil. Using a rubber spatula, mix until the liquid is absorbed and the ingredients form a sticky dough ball. Cover the bowl with a damp tea towel or plastic wrap and set aside in a warm spot to rise for 1 to 1½ hours, until the dough has doubled in bulk.

2. Set a rack in the middle of the oven and preheat it to 425°F. Grease two 1-quart oven-safe bowls with the softened butter—be generous. Using two forks, deflate the dough by releasing it from the sides of the bowl and pulling it toward the center. Rotate the bowl quarter turns as you deflate, turning the mass into a rough ball.

3. Using your two forks and working from the center out, separate the dough into two equal pieces. Use the forks to lift each half of dough into a prepared bowl. If the dough is too wet to transfer with forks, lightly grease your hands with butter or oil, then transfer each half to a bowl. Do not cover the bowls. Let the dough rise on the countertop near the oven (or another warm, draft-free spot) for 10 to 20 minutes, until the top of the dough just crowns the rims of the bowls.

4. Transfer the bowls to the oven and bake for 15 minutes. Reduce the heat to 375°F and bake for 17 to 20 minutes more, until golden all around. Remove the bowls from the oven and turn the loaves out onto cooling racks. If the loaves look pale, return them to their bowls and bake for 5 minutes longer. Let the loaves cool for 15 minutes before cutting.

EINKORN BREAD
WITH SESAME, ONION, AND CHIVES

MAKES 2 LOAVES

Einkorn, an ancient wheat, lacks certain gluten proteins found in conventional wheat, allowing many people with gluten sensitivities to tolerate it (though not those with celiac disease). Carla Bartolucci, author of *Einkorn: Recipes for Nature's Original Wheat*, discovered the near-extinct grain while researching her daughter's wheat intolerance. When she saw her daughter's health improve dramatically upon eliminating all wheat except einkorn, Carla began working with farmers near her home in northern Italy to find and replenish seeds for planting. Today, these farmers are the largest group of growers of einkorn in the world. The flour can be found in most natural foods markets, and Carla's company, Jovial Foods, sells an organic line online.

3 tablespoons neutral oil

2 cups diced onions (about 2 medium onions)

2 teaspoons plus a pinch of kosher salt

2 tablespoons sesame seeds

4 cups (512 g) unbleached all-purpose einkorn flour

2 teaspoons sugar

2¼ teaspoons instant yeast

¼ cup chopped fresh chives

2 cups lukewarm water

Softened unsalted butter, for greasing

1. In a large skillet over high heat, place 1 tablespoon of the oil. When it begins to shimmer, add the onions and immediately reduce the heat to low. Add a generous pinch of salt and let the onions cook, stirring occasionally, for 20 minutes, or until golden. Remove the pan from the heat and set aside to cool.

2. Meanwhile, in a medium skillet over medium heat, toast the sesame seeds, stirring, until golden, about 5 minutes. Transfer to a plate to cool.

3. In a large bowl, whisk together the flour, 2 teaspoons salt, sugar, instant yeast, chives, onions, and toasted sesame seeds. Add the water, followed by the remaining 2 tablespoons oil. Using a rubber spatula, mix until the liquid is absorbed and the ingredients form a sticky dough ball. Cover the bowl with a damp tea towel or plastic wrap and set aside in a warm spot to rise for 1 to 1½ hours, until the dough has doubled in bulk.

4. Set a rack in the middle of the oven and preheat it to 375°F. Grease two 1-quart oven-safe bowls with the softened butter—be generous. Using two forks, deflate the dough by releasing it from the sides of the bowl and pulling it toward the center. Rotate the bowl quarter turns as you deflate, turning the mass into a rough ball.

5. Using two large mixing spoons and working from the center out, separate the dough into two equal pieces. Using greased hands or two large spoons, lift each half of dough into a prepared bowl. Do not cover the bowls. Let the dough rise on the countertop near the oven (or another warm, draft-free spot) for 10 to 20 minutes, until the top of the dough just crowns the rims of the bowls.

6. Transfer the bowls to the oven and bake for 40 minutes, or until golden all around. Remove the bowls from the oven and turn the loaves out onto cooling racks. If the loaves look pale, return them to their bowls and bake for 5 minutes longer. Let the loaves cool for 15 minutes before cutting.

BEER BREAD
WITH GOLDEN RAISINS AND WALNUTS

MAKES 2 LOAVES

Beer most often is used as a substitute for water in quick breads (which are leavened by baking soda or baking powder) to provide a yeasty flavor, but it can be used in yeasted breads, too. During baking, although the alcohol cooks off, the flavor of the beer persists, imparting the finished loaves with a slight sourness—in a good way. Here, sweet golden raisins offset this tang, and walnuts provide crunch and body. Day old, this makes excellent open-faced sandwiches with Cheddar cheese and lingonberry jam.

1½ cups (170 g) walnuts

4 cups (512 g) unbleached all-purpose flour

2 teaspoons kosher salt

1 tablespoon sugar

2¼ teaspoons instant yeast

½ cup (92 g) golden raisins

1½ cups amber ale, room temperature

½ cup boiling water

¼ cup neutral oil

Softened unsalted butter, for greasing

1. Preheat the oven to 350°F. Lay the walnuts on a sheet pan, spreading them in a single layer. Toast in the oven for about 10 minutes, or until lightly golden. Remove and transfer the walnuts to a clean tea towel and rub to remove the walnut skins. Taking care to leave as many skins behind as possible, transfer the nuts to a colander and shake to remove any remaining skins. Set aside.

2. In a large bowl, whisk together the flour, salt, sugar, and instant yeast. Add the toasted walnuts, breaking up any large pieces with your hands, and golden raisins. In a small bowl, combine the beer and boiling water, followed by the oil, and add it to the flour. Using a rubber spatula, mix until the liquid is absorbed and the ingredients form a sticky dough ball. Cover the bowl with a damp tea towel or plastic wrap and set aside in a warm spot to rise for 1 to 1½ hours, until the dough has doubled in bulk.

3. Set a rack in the middle of the oven and preheat it to 425°F. Grease two 1-quart oven-safe bowls with the softened butter—be generous. Using two forks, deflate the dough by releasing it from the sides of the bowl and pulling it toward the center. Rotate the bowl quarter turns as you deflate, turning the mass into a rough ball.

4. Using your two forks and working from the center out, separate the dough into two equal pieces. Use the forks to lift each half of dough into a prepared bowl. If the dough is too wet to transfer with forks, lightly grease your hands with butter or oil, then transfer each half to a bowl. Do not cover the bowls. Let the dough rise on the countertop near the oven (or another warm, draft-free spot) for 10 to 20 minutes, until the top of the dough just crowns the rims of the bowls.

5. Transfer the bowls to the oven and bake for 15 minutes. Reduce the heat to 375°F and bake for 17 to 20 minutes more, until golden all around. Remove the bowls from the oven and turn the loaves out onto cooling racks. If the loaves look pale, return them to their bowls and bake for 5 minutes longer. Let the loaves cool for 15 minutes before cutting.

WALNUT BREAD

MAKES 2 LOAVES

A partially whole-wheat dough and a generous amount of toasted walnuts make this a sturdy *boule*, ideal for a fruit and cheese plate or an open-faced sandwich, like the Leek, Ham, and Emmental Croque Madame (page 133), beside a spring greens salad. Walnut oil enhances the rich flavor of the toasted nuts, but olive or grapeseed oil works fine, too.

1½ cups (170 g) walnuts

3 cups (384 g) unbleached all-purpose flour

1 cup (128 g) whole-wheat flour

2 teaspoons kosher salt

2 teaspoons sugar

2½ teaspoons instant yeast

2 cups lukewarm water

¼ cup walnut oil

Softened unsalted butter, for greasing

1. Preheat the oven to 350°F. Lay the walnuts on a sheet pan, spreading them in a single layer. Toast them in the oven for about 10 minutes, or until lightly golden. Remove and transfer the walnuts to a clean tea towel and rub to remove their skins. Taking care to leave as many skins behind as possible, transfer the nuts to a colander and shake to remove any remaining skins.

2. In a large bowl, whisk together the flours, salt, sugar, and instant yeast. Add the toasted walnuts, breaking up any large pieces with your hands, and toss to coat. Add the water, followed by the oil. Using a rubber spatula, mix until the liquid is absorbed and the ingredients form a sticky dough ball. Cover the bowl with a damp tea towel or plastic wrap and set aside in a warm spot to rise for 1 to 1½ hours, until the dough has doubled in bulk.

3. Set a rack in the middle of the oven and preheat it to 425°F. Grease two 1-quart oven-safe bowls with the softened butter—be generous. Using two forks, deflate the dough by releasing it from the sides of the bowl and pulling it toward the center. Rotate the bowl quarter turns as you deflate, turning the mass into a rough ball.

4. Using your two forks and working from the center out, separate the dough into two equal pieces. Use the forks to lift each half of dough into a prepared bowl. If the dough is too wet to transfer with forks, lightly grease your hands with butter or oil, then transfer each half to a bowl. Do not cover the bowls. Let the dough rise on the countertop near the oven (or another warm, draft-free spot) for 10 to 20 minutes, until the top of the dough just crowns the rims of the bowls.

5. Transfer the bowls to the oven and bake for 15 minutes. Reduce the heat to 375°F and bake for 17 to 20 minutes more, until golden all around. Remove the bowls from the oven and turn the loaves out onto cooling racks. If the loaves look pale, return them to their bowls and bake for 5 minutes longer. Let the loaves cool for 15 minutes before cutting.

HONEY WHOLE-WHEAT BREAD

MAKES 2 LOAVES

Despite the impression I may have created thus far, my mother isn't a one-trick pony. She bakes all sorts of breads, and when my siblings and I were younger, many came from the *Bakery Lane Soup Bowl*, by Marge Mitchell and Joan Sedgwick, her paperback edition now bound by rubber bands, the pages tattered and stained from years of use. Inspired by a favorite recipe in that book, this bread has great texture—a nice chew, thanks to the honey, and slight crunch, thanks to the cornmeal. *The Bakery Lane* recipe uses strong coffee, which darkens the crumb and imparts a subtle bitterness. If you have some coffee left in the pot, use as much as ½ cup in place of the water. Sliced, toasted, and smeared with butter, this is a perfect everyday breakfast bread.

2 cups (256 g) unbleached all-purpose flour

2 cups (256 g) whole-wheat flour

⅓ cup (55 g) medium-grind cornmeal

2 teaspoons kosher salt

2¼ teaspoons instant yeast

½ cup boiling water

¼ cup honey

Softened unsalted butter, for greasing

1. In a large bowl, whisk together the flours, cornmeal, salt, and instant yeast. In a separate small bowl, pour the boiling water over the honey and stir to dissolve. Add 1½ cups water and stir to combine. Add the honey mixture to the flour. Using a rubber spatula, mix until the liquid is absorbed and the ingredients form a sticky dough ball. Cover the bowl with a damp tea towel or plastic wrap and set aside in a warm spot to rise for 1 to 1½ hours, until the dough has doubled in bulk.

2. Set a rack in the middle of the oven and preheat it to 375°F. Grease two 1-quart oven-safe bowls with the softened butter—be generous. Using two forks, deflate the dough by releasing it from the sides of the bowl and pulling it toward the center. Rotate the bowl quarter turns as you deflate, turning the mass into a rough ball.

3. Using your two forks and working from the center out, separate the dough into two equal pieces. Use the forks to lift each half of dough into a prepared bowl. If the dough is too wet to transfer with forks, lightly grease your hands with butter or oil, then transfer each half to a bowl. Do not cover the bowls. Let the dough rise on the countertop near the oven (or another warm, draft-free spot) for 10 to 20 minutes, until the top of the dough just crowns the rims of the bowls.

4. Transfer the bowls to the oven and bake for 40 minutes, or until golden all around. Remove the bowls from the oven and turn the loaves out onto cooling racks. If the loaves look pale, return them to their bowls and bake for 5 minutes longer. Let the loaves cool for 15 minutes before cutting.

ANADAMA BREAD

The story goes like this: Long ago in Massachusetts, a fisherman, tired of the cornmeal mush his wife, Anna, would pack for his daily lunch, took matters into his own hands. While cursing, "Anna, damn her!" he added yeast and molasses to his mush, tossed it in the oven, and baked what turned out to be a legendary loaf.

Though lore surrounds its name, anadamas consistently include two ingredients: briefly cooked cornmeal and a healthy dose of molasses, which stains the crumb gingerbread brown and makes it slightly sweet. Whole-wheat or rye flour often makes up a portion of the dough, too.

The anadama method—soften grains in boiling water, then mix with a blend of white and whole-wheat flours—inspired the three breads that follow this one: oatmeal-maple (see page 41), multigrain (see page 42), and bulgur (see page 43). The resulting loaves are heartier than many of the other breads in this chapter, each grain imparting the loaves with nuanced flavor and texture.

½ cup (93 g) medium-grind cornmeal

1 cup boiling water

2 tablespoons (¼ stick) unsalted butter, plus more, softened, for greasing

¼ cup molasses

1 cup lukewarm water

2¼ cups (288 g) unbleached all-purpose flour

1 cup (128 g) whole-wheat flour

2 teaspoons kosher salt

2¼ teaspoons instant yeast

1. In a medium bowl, place the cornmeal. Pour the boiling water over it. Add the 2 tablespoons butter and molasses and stir to combine. Let it stand for 30 minutes. Add the lukewarm water and stir to combine.

2. In a large bowl, whisk together the flours, salt, and instant yeast. Add the cornmeal mixture. Using a rubber spatula, mix until the liquid is absorbed and the ingredients form a sticky dough ball. Cover the bowl with a damp tea towel or plastic wrap and set aside in a warm spot to rise for 1 to 1½ hours, until the dough has doubled in bulk.

3. Set a rack in the middle of the oven and preheat it to 375°F. Grease two 1-quart oven-safe bowls with the softened butter—be generous. Using two forks, deflate the dough by releasing it from the sides of the bowl and pulling it toward the center. Rotate the bowl quarter turns as you deflate, turning the mass into a rough ball.

4. Using your two forks and working from the center out, separate the dough into two equal pieces. Use the forks to lift each half of dough into a prepared bowl. If the dough is too wet to transfer with forks, lightly grease your hands with butter or oil, then transfer each half to a bowl. Do not cover the bowls. Let the dough rise on the countertop near the oven (or another warm, draft-free spot) for 10 to 20 minutes, until the top of the dough just crowns the rims of the bowls.

5. Transfer the bowls to the oven and bake for 40 minutes, or until golden all around. Remove the bowls from the oven and turn the loaves out onto cooling racks. If the loaves look pale, return them to their bowls and bake for 5 minutes longer. Let the loaves cool for 15 minutes before cutting.

OATMEAL-MAPLE BREAD

MAKES 2 LOAVES

I usually leave San Francisco dreaming about morning buns, the buttery, flaky, cinnamon-swirled breakfast treat available at every turn. But my most recent visit, which led me to The Mill—Josey Baker Bread and Four Barrel Coffee's joint bakery and café—left me fixated on toast, thick slices of it, topped simply but generously: dark mountain rye, for instance, with swirls of cream cheese, salt, and pepper, or, my favorite, oat porridge bread, spread with butter and doused with maple syrup, like French toast that skipped the custard soak. Here, the oats and the maple unite in the bread itself, which is not to say a slice of it wouldn't welcome a drizzle more of syrup on top. This loaf is chewy, slightly sweet, and sturdy, and while it is particularly nice in the morning, it pairs well with sharp Cheddar cheese for an afternoon snack. No need to use fancy maple syrup—lower grades, in fact, add a more pronounced flavor.

1 cup (95 g) rolled oats

1 cup boiling water

¼ cup maple syrup

2¼ cups (288 g) unbleached all-purpose flour

1 cup (128 g) whole-wheat flour

2 teaspoons kosher salt

2¼ teaspoons instant yeast

Softened unsalted butter, for greasing

1. In a small bowl, combine the oats, boiling water, and maple syrup. Let stand for 10 minutes. Add 1 cup water and stir to combine.

2. In a large bowl, whisk together the flours, salt, and instant yeast. Add the oat mixture. Using a rubber spatula, mix until the liquid is absorbed and the ingredients form a sticky dough ball. Cover the bowl with a damp tea towel or plastic wrap and set aside in a warm spot to rise for 1 to 1½ hours, until the dough has doubled in bulk.

3. Set a rack in the middle of the oven and preheat it to 375°F. Grease two 1-quart oven-safe bowls with the softened butter—be generous. Using two forks, deflate the dough by releasing it from the sides of the bowl and pulling it toward the center. Rotate the bowl quarter turns as you deflate, turning the mass into a rough ball.

4. Using your two forks and working from the center out, separate the dough into two equal pieces. Use the forks to lift each half of dough into a prepared bowl. If the dough is too wet to transfer with forks, lightly grease your hands with butter or oil, then transfer each half to a bowl. Do not cover the bowls. Let the dough rise on the countertop near the oven (or another warm, draft-free spot) for 10 to 20 minutes, until the top of the dough just crowns the rims of the bowls.

5. Transfer the bowls to the oven and bake for 40 minutes, or until golden all around. Remove the bowls from the oven and turn the loaves out onto cooling racks. If the loaves look pale, return them to their bowls and bake for 5 minutes longer. Let the loaves cool for 15 minutes before cutting.

MULTIGRAIN CEREAL BREAD

MAKES 2 LOAVES

If hot cereal frequents your breakfast routine, this bread, made with a 10-grain blend, will taste familiar: hearty yet healthy, ever so slightly improved by a pat of butter and a sprinkling of cinnamon and sugar. For busy mornings or breakfast on the fly, thick slices of this fiber-filled bread, toasted and slathered with almond butter (see page 117), are a godsend, at once healthy and nourishing. You can vary the sweetener to your liking—honey or molasses works well—and if you like dried fruit, throw in ½ cup of raisins or dried cranberries. Be sure to look for *hot* cereal blends, such as Bob's Red Mill 7-, 8-, or 10-Grain Cereal.

⅔ cup (106 g) 10-grain hot cereal

1 cup boiling water

¼ cup maple syrup

2¼ cups (288 g) unbleached all-purpose flour

1 cup (128 g) whole-wheat flour

2 teaspoons kosher salt

2¼ teaspoons instant yeast

Softened unsalted butter, for greasing

1. In a medium bowl, combine the cereal, boiling water, and maple syrup. Let stand for 10 minutes. Add 1 cup water and stir to combine.

2. In a large bowl, whisk together the flours, salt, and instant yeast. Add the cereal mixture. Using a rubber spatula, mix until the liquid is absorbed and the ingredients form a sticky dough ball. Cover the bowl with a damp tea towel or plastic wrap and set aside in a warm spot to rise for 1 to 1½ hours, until the dough has doubled in bulk.

3. Set a rack in the middle of the oven and preheat it to 375°F. Grease two 1-quart oven-safe bowls with the softened butter—be generous. Using two forks, deflate the dough by releasing it from the sides of the bowl and pulling it toward the center. Rotate the bowl quarter turns as you deflate, turning the mass into a rough ball.

4. Using your two forks and working from the center out, separate the dough into two equal pieces. Use the forks to lift each half of dough into a prepared bowl. If the dough is too wet to transfer with forks, lightly grease your hands with butter or oil, then transfer each half to a bowl. Do not cover the bowls. Let the dough rise on the countertop near the oven (or another warm, draft-free spot) for 10 to 20 minutes, until the top of the dough just crowns the rims of the bowls.

5. Transfer the bowls to the oven and bake for 40 minutes, or until golden all around. Remove the bowls from the oven and turn the loaves out onto cooling racks. If the loaves look pale, return them to their bowls and bake for 5 minutes longer. Let the loaves cool for 15 minutes before cutting.

BULGUR BREAD

Prized for its nutritional value and quick cooking time, bulgur, a whole-grain wheat that has been parboiled, dried, and cracked, has been a staple of the eastern Mediterranean for thousands of years. It evokes tabbouleh and kibbeh, but it can be added to bread, too, lending a pleasantly chewy texture while amping up the fiber and complex carbohydrates, which keep us sated longer. Any variety of bulgur will work here: Bob's Red Mill bulgur (red or golden) is widely available; medium-coarse Turkish bulgur can be found in Middle Eastern markets.

1 cup boiling water

½ cup (100 g) bulgur

¼ cup honey or maple syrup

1 cup lukewarm water

2¼ cups (288 g) unbleached all-purpose flour

1 cup (128 g) whole-wheat flour

2 teaspoons kosher salt

2¼ teaspoons instant yeast

Softened unsalted butter, for greasing

1. In a small bowl, pour the boiling water over the bulgur. Add the honey. Let stand for 30 minutes. Add the lukewarm water and stir to combine.

2. In a large bowl, whisk together the flours, salt, and instant yeast. Add the bulgur mixture. Using a rubber spatula, mix until the liquid is absorbed and the ingredients form a sticky dough ball. Cover the bowl with a damp tea towel or plastic wrap and set aside in a warm spot to rise for 1 to 1½ hours, until the dough has doubled in bulk.

3. Set a rack in the middle of the oven and preheat it to 375°F. Grease two 1-quart oven-safe bowls with the softened butter—be generous. Using two forks, deflate the dough by releasing it from the sides of the bowl and pulling it toward the center. Rotate the bowl quarter turns as you deflate, turning the mass into a rough ball.

4. Using your two forks and working from the center out, separate the dough into two equal pieces. Use the forks to lift each half of dough into a prepared bowl. If the dough is too wet to transfer with forks, lightly grease your hands with butter or oil, then transfer each half to a bowl. Do not cover the bowls. Let the dough rise on the countertop near the oven (or other warm, draft-free spot) for 10 to 20 minutes, until the top of the dough just crowns the rim of the bowls.

5. Transfer the bowls to the oven and bake for 40 minutes, or until golden all around. Remove the bowls from the oven and turn the loaves out onto cooling racks. If the loaves look pale, return them to their bowls and bake for 5 minutes longer. Let the loaves cool for 15 minutes before cutting.

KALAMATA OLIVE BREAD

Inspired by a favorite recipe in Diane Kochilas's *Glorious Foods of Greece*, this bread incorporates grated onions, whose sweetness offsets the saltiness of the olives. Serve this festive *boule* with an array of *mezethes*—roasted red peppers, feta, *taramosalata*, *tiropitas*, or lamb meatballs (see page 230)—or spread it with Tzatziki (page 194) and sandwich it with thin slices of roasted lamb. Fresh thyme or dried oregano can be substituted for the rosemary.

4 cups (512 g) unbleached all-purpose flour

2 teaspoons kosher salt

2 teaspoons sugar

2¼ teaspoons instant yeast

2 teaspoons finely minced fresh rosemary

¾ cup (115 g) chopped pitted kalamata olives

½ cup (65 g) finely chopped sweet onion

2 cups lukewarm water

¼ cup neutral oil

Softened unsalted butter, for greasing

1. In a large bowl, whisk together the flour, salt, sugar, instant yeast, and rosemary. Add the olives and onions, and toss to coat. Add the water, followed by the oil. Using a rubber spatula, mix until the liquid is absorbed and the ingredients form a sticky dough ball. Cover the bowl with a damp tea towel or plastic wrap and set aside in a warm spot to rise for 1 to 1½ hours, until the dough has doubled in bulk.

2. Set a rack in the middle of the oven and preheat it to 425°F. Grease two 1-quart oven-safe bowls with the softened butter—be generous. Using two forks, deflate the dough by releasing it from the sides of the bowl and pulling it toward the center. Rotate the bowl quarter turns as you deflate, turning the mass into a rough ball.

3. Using your two forks and working from the center out, separate the dough into two equal pieces. Use the forks to lift each half of dough into a prepared bowl. If the dough is too wet to transfer with forks, lightly grease your hands with butter or oil, then transfer each half to a bowl. Do not cover the bowls. Let the dough rise on the countertop near the oven (or another warm, draft-free spot) for 10 to 20 minutes, until the top of the dough just crowns the rims of the bowls.

4. Transfer the bowls to the oven and bake for 15 minutes. Reduce the heat to 375°F and bake for 17 to 20 minutes more, until golden all around. Remove the bowls from the oven and turn the loaves out onto cooling racks. If the loaves look pale, return them to their bowls and bake for 5 minutes longer. Let the loaves cool for 15 minutes before cutting.

APPLE, ALMOND, AND THYME BREAD

MAKES 2 LOAVES

By infusing milk with thyme here, this bread's herbal flavor is more diffuse than it would be by simply adding chopped thyme to the dough. Roasted apples with sugar make this a slightly sweeter loaf, though by no means should it be relegated to dessert. The subtly pervasive scent makes it as well suited for a roast pork dinner as for a bacon-and-egg breakfast.

2 cups (255 g) ¾-inch-cubed and peeled apples (see Note)

4 tablespoons neutral oil (although almond oil is nice, if you have it)

4 tablespoons (55 g) sugar

½ cup (48 g) sliced almonds

2 cups 2 percent or whole milk

10 sprigs of fresh thyme

4 cups (512 g) unbleached all-purpose flour

2 teaspoons kosher salt

2¼ teaspoons instant yeast

1 teaspoon vanilla extract or paste

Softened unsalted butter, for greasing

1. Set a rack in the middle of the oven and preheat it to 425°F. In a small bowl, toss the cubed apple with 1 tablespoon of the oil and 2 tablespoons of the sugar. Arrange the apples on a sheet pan, spreading them in a single layer. Transfer to the oven and roast for 10 minutes until tender when pierced with a knife. Remove from the oven and set aside. Turn off the oven.

2. In a medium skillet, toast the almonds over medium heat, stirring, until they begin to turn golden, 3 to 5 minutes. Transfer to a plate to cool.

3. In a small saucepan, heat 1 cup of the milk over high heat until it comes to a boil, about 3 minutes. Remove the pan from the burner and immediately add the thyme sprigs. Steep for 10 minutes. Remove and discard the thyme sprigs and add the remaining cup of milk to the pan.

4. In a large bowl, whisk together the flour, salt, instant yeast, and remaining 2 tablespoons of sugar. Add the cooled almonds and toss to coat. Add the roasted apples and any collected juices, and toss to combine.

5. Pour the milk into the flour, followed by the remaining 3 tablespoons oil and vanilla. Using a rubber spatula, mix until the liquid is absorbed and the ingredients form a sticky dough ball. Cover the bowl with a damp tea towel or plastic wrap and set aside in a warm spot to rise for 1½ to 2 hours, or until the dough has doubled in bulk.

6. Preheat the oven to 375°F. Grease two 1-quart oven-safe bowls with the softened butter—be generous. Using two forks, deflate the dough by

releasing it from the sides of the bowl and pulling it toward the center. Rotate the bowl quarter turns as you deflate, turning the mass into a rough ball.

7. Using your two forks and working from the center out, separate the dough into two equal pieces. Use the forks to lift each half of dough into a prepared bowl. If the dough is too wet to transfer with forks, lightly grease your hands with butter or oil, then transfer each half to a bowl. Do not cover the bowls. Let the dough rise on the countertop near the oven (or another warm, draft-free spot) for 10 to 20 minutes, until the top of the dough just crowns the rims of the bowls.

8. Transfer the bowls to the oven and bake for 35 minutes, or until golden all around. Remove the bowls from the oven and turn the loaves out onto cooling racks. If the loaves look pale, return them to their bowls and bake for 5 minutes longer. Let the loaves cool for 15 minutes before cutting.

NOTE: Apples such as Jonagold, Winesap, Cortland, Northern Spy, Granny Smith, Honey Crisp, Mutsu, or Fuji are all good choices—use whatever you like best.

RYE BREAD

MAKES 2 LOAVES

Pastrami, corned beef, tuna salad, cured salmon—
many a sandwich filling excels when flanked
by tangy slices of rye bread. On its own, rye, a
low-gluten grain, makes for a dense loaf, which
is why many rye breads are made with a mix of
all-purpose and whole-wheat flours. Even in small
quantities, however, rye's strong, acidic flavor
prevails. Add ½ cup of finely grated onion for a
slightly sweeter loaf.

3 cups (384 g) unbleached all-purpose flour

1 cup (128 g) rye or pumpernickel flour

2 teaspoons kosher salt

2¼ teaspoons instant yeast

1 tablespoon caraway seeds

1 tablespoon honey or molasses

2 cups lukewarm water

¼ cup neutral oil

Softened unsalted butter, for greasing

1. In a large bowl, whisk together the flours, salt, instant yeast, and caraway seeds. Dissolve the honey in the water, then add it to the flour, followed by the oil. Using a rubber spatula, mix until the liquid is absorbed and the ingredients form a sticky dough ball. Cover the bowl with a damp tea towel or plastic wrap and set aside in a warm spot to rise for 1 to 1½ hours, until the dough has doubled in bulk.

2. Set a rack in the middle of the oven and preheat it to 425°F. Grease two 1-quart oven-safe bowls with the softened butter—be generous. Using two forks, deflate the dough by releasing it from the sides of the bowl and pulling it toward the center. Rotate the bowl quarter turns as you deflate, turning the mass into a rough ball.

3. Using your two forks and working from the center out, separate the dough into two equal pieces. Use the forks to lift each half of dough into a prepared bowl. If the dough is too wet to transfer with forks, lightly grease your hands with butter or oil, then transfer each half to a bowl. Do not cover the bowls. Let the dough rise on the countertop near the oven (or another warm, draft-free spot) for 10 to 20 minutes, until the top of the dough just crowns the rims of the bowls.

4. Transfer the bowls to the oven and bake for 15 minutes. Reduce the heat to 375°F and bake for 17 to 20 minutes more, until golden all around. Remove the bowls from the oven and turn the loaves out onto cooling racks. If the loaves look pale, return them to their bowls and bake for 5 minutes longer. Let the loaves cool for 15 minutes before cutting.

ROASTED GARLIC BREAD

MAKES 2 LOAVES

Roasting whole heads of garlic tames their bite, somehow both mellowing and intensifying the flavor. Mashed into a creamy purée, the caramelized cloves permeate these loaves, making them sweet and aromatic. The heads of garlic roast for about an hour, but they can be made up to three days in advance and stored in the refrigerator in an airtight container. In addition to flavoring this bread, the roasted garlic purée can be stirred into hummus, swirled into soups, mashed into potatoes, or simply spread across toast like butter, with a pinch of sea salt.

4 cups (512 g) unbleached all-purpose flour

2 teaspoons kosher salt

2 teaspoons sugar

2¼ teaspoons instant yeast

1 teaspoon finely chopped fresh rosemary

2 teaspoons finely chopped fresh thyme

2 cups lukewarm water

¼ cup neutral oil

Roasted Garlic Purée (recipe follows)

Softened unsalted butter, for greasing

1. In a large bowl, whisk together the flour, salt, sugar, instant yeast, rosemary, and thyme. Add the water followed by the oil and the roasted garlic purée. Using a rubber spatula, mix until the liquid is absorbed and the ingredients form a sticky dough ball. Cover the bowl with a damp tea towel or plastic wrap and set aside in a warm spot to rise for 1 to 1½ hours, until the dough has doubled in bulk.

2. Set a rack in the middle of the oven and preheat it to 425°F. Grease two 1-quart oven-safe bowls with the softened butter—be generous. Using two forks, deflate the dough by releasing it from the sides of the bowl and pulling it toward the center. Rotate the bowl quarter turns as you deflate, turning the mass into a rough ball.

3. Using your two forks and working from the center out, separate the dough into two equal pieces. Use the forks to lift each half of dough into a prepared bowl. If the dough is too wet to transfer with forks, lightly grease your hands with butter or oil, then transfer each half to a bowl. Do not cover the bowls. Let the dough rise on the countertop near the oven (or another warm, draft-free spot) for 10 to 20 minutes, until the top of the dough just crowns the rims of the bowls.

4. Transfer the bowls to the oven and bake for 15 minutes. Reduce the heat to 375°F and bake for 17 to 20 minutes more, until golden all around. Remove the bowls from the oven and turn the loaves out onto cooling racks. If the loaves look pale, return them to their bowls and bake for 5 minutes longer. Let the loaves cool for 15 minutes before cutting.

(recipe continues)

Roasted Garlic Purée

MAKES ¼ TO ⅓ CUP

2 heads of garlic

2 tablespoons extra-virgin olive oil

Kosher salt

1. Preheat the oven to 400°F. Cut off the very top portion of each head of garlic to reveal just a few cloves. Place each head on its own large sheet of aluminum foil and drizzle each with a tablespoon of oil and season with a pinch of salt. Curl up the edges of the foil to create rims, then pour 2 tablespoons of water around each head of garlic. Wrap up the foil into pouches, making sure they are sealed.

2. Place the pouches on a sheet pan, transfer to the oven, and roast for 1 hour. Remove the pouches from the oven and let cool for a few minutes before carefully opening them (steam will pour out). When the garlic is cool enough to handle, squeeze each clove out of its paper sheath onto a plate. Mash into a purée using the back of a fork. The purée can be stored in an airtight container in the refrigerator for up to 3 days.

CHEESY CHEDDAR AND PARMIGIANO BREAD

MAKES 2 LOAVES

A healthy measure of Cheddar and Parmigiano-Reggiano combine in this moist and fragrant loaf, as much a treat freshly baked as day old: layered with more cheese, this loaf makes a superlative grilled cheese (see page 128); toasted and topped with leeks and ham, a memorable croque madame (see page 133); cubed, tossed with oil, and roasted, irresistible croutons. These loaves require a long cooling to allow for beneficial carryover cooking, so be sure to plan ahead.

4 cups (512 g) unbleached all-purpose flour

2 teaspoons kosher salt

2 teaspoons sugar

2½ teaspoons instant yeast

⅛ teaspoon cayenne pepper (optional)

1½ cups (170 g) grated Cheddar cheese, lightly packed

Heaping ½ cup (57 g) grated Parmigiano-Reggiano

2 cups lukewarm water

Dash of hot sauce, such as Tabasco (optional)

Softened unsalted butter, for greasing

1. In a large bowl, whisk together the flour, salt, sugar, instant yeast, and cayenne, if using. Add the cheeses and toss to coat. Add the water and the hot sauce, if using. Using a rubber spatula, mix until the liquid is absorbed and the ingredients form a sticky dough ball. Cover the bowl with a damp tea towel or plastic wrap and set aside in a warm spot to rise for 1 to 1½ hours, until the dough has doubled in bulk.

2. Set a rack in the middle of the oven and preheat it to 375°F. Grease two 1-quart oven-safe bowls with the softened butter—be generous. Using two forks, deflate the dough by releasing it from the sides of the bowl and pulling it toward the center. Rotate the bowl quarter turns as you deflate, turning the mass into a rough ball.

3. Using your two forks and working from the center out, separate the dough into two equal pieces. Use the forks to lift each half of dough into a prepared bowl. If the dough is too wet to transfer with forks, lightly grease your hands with butter or oil, then transfer each half to a bowl. Do not cover the bowls. Let the dough rise on the countertop near the oven (or another warm, draft-free spot) for 10 to 20 minutes, until the top of the dough just crowns the rims of the bowls.

4. Transfer the bowls to the oven and bake for 45 minutes, or until golden all around. Remove the bowls from the oven and turn the loaves out onto cooling racks. If the loaves look pale, return them to their bowls and bake for 5 minutes longer. Let the loaves cool for 30 minutes before cutting.

POTATO BREAD

Mashed potatoes incorporated into bread dough give bounce and softness to the finished crumb. The mixed dough may feel denser than some of the others here, but in the oven, the potato expands, causing the loaves to rise dramatically. The taste of the potato is nearly indiscernible in the loaf, though its moist springiness distinguishes it. Dill seed will impart an earthy, herbal freshness, or you can use caraway instead, if you prefer. Note that this loaf benefits from a long cooling, which allows it to finish cooking as it rests.

1 medium russet potato (6 to 7 ounces), peeled and cubed

2 tablespoons (¼ stick) unsalted butter, melted

4 cups (512 g) unbleached all-purpose flour

2 teaspoons kosher salt

1 tablespoon sugar

2¼ teaspoons instant yeast

2 teaspoons whole dill seed

Softened unsalted butter, for greasing

1. In a medium saucepan set over medium heat, cover the potato with at least 3 cups of water. Simmer until completely tender, 15 to 20 minutes. Transfer the potato, reserving the cooking liquid, to a medium bowl and mash until smooth. Measure out ½ cup of the potatoes and set aside. Reserve the remainder for another use.

2. In a medium bowl, pour 2 cups of the reserved potato cooking water. Add the ½ cup mashed potato and the melted butter and stir until smooth. Let the mixture cool until lukewarm, about 30 minutes.

3. In a large bowl, whisk together the flour, salt, sugar, instant yeast, and dill seed. Add the potato mixture. Using a rubber spatula, mix until the liquid is absorbed and the ingredients form a sticky dough ball. Cover the bowl with a damp tea towel or plastic wrap and set aside in a warm spot to rise for 1 to 1½ hours, until the dough has doubled in bulk.

4. Set a rack in the middle of the oven and preheat it to 375°F. Grease two 1-quart oven-safe bowls with the softened butter—be generous. Using two forks, deflate the dough by releasing it from the sides of the bowl and pulling it toward the center. Rotate the bowl quarter turns as you deflate, turning the mass into a rough ball.

5. Using your two forks and working from the center out, separate the dough into two equal pieces. Use the forks to lift each half of dough into a prepared bowl. If the dough is too wet to transfer with forks, lightly grease your hands with butter or oil, then transfer each half to a bowl. Do not cover the bowls. Let the dough rise on the countertop near the oven (or another warm, draft-free spot) for 10 to 20 minutes, until the top of the dough just crowns the rims of the bowls.

6. Transfer the bowls to the oven and bake for 40 to 45 minutes, or until the loaves are deep golden all around. Remove the bowls from the oven and turn the loaves out onto cooling racks. If the loaves look pale, return them to their bowls and bake for 5 minutes longer. Let the loaves cool for at least 30 minutes before cutting.

NOTE: Try this variation: use sweet potato in place of the potato, brown sugar in place of the white sugar, and melted coconut oil in place of the melted butter.

SPICY JALAPEÑO, CORN, AND JACK BREAD

MAKES 2 LOAVES

These loaves emerge from the oven beautifully golden and crisp, thanks to a heap of Monterey Jack cheese. Cornmeal gives the crumb both creaminess and crunch. The degree of spiciness can be tailored to your liking by removing or including the jalapeño's white pith, but even when stripped of its spicy membranes, the pepper's flavor still permeates. Slice, toast, and top with smashed avocado or soft scrambled eggs and salsa. Note that these loaves benefit from a slightly longer cooling because of the heft of the cheese, jalapeño, and scallions.

4 cups (512 g) unbleached all-purpose flour

⅓ cup (55 g) medium-grind cornmeal

2 teaspoons kosher salt

2 teaspoons sugar

2½ teaspoons instant yeast

2 cups (170 g) lightly packed grated Monterey Jack cheese (see Note)

1 jalapeño or serrano pepper, finely diced, seeded, if desired

½ cup sliced scallions, white and green parts

2 cups lukewarm water

Softened unsalted butter, for greasing

1. In a large bowl, whisk together the flour, cornmeal, salt, sugar, and instant yeast. Add the cheese, pepper, and scallions, and toss to coat. Add the water. Using a rubber spatula, mix until the liquid is absorbed and the ingredients form a sticky dough ball. Cover the bowl with a damp tea towel or plastic wrap and set aside in a warm spot to rise for 1 to 1½ hours, until the dough has doubled in bulk.

2. Set a rack in the middle of the oven and preheat it to 375°F. Grease two 1-quart oven-safe bowls with the softened butter—be generous. Using two forks, deflate the dough by releasing it from the sides of the bowl and pulling it toward the center. Rotate the bowl quarter turns as you deflate, turning the mass into a rough ball.

3. Using your two forks and working from the center out, separate the dough into two equal pieces. Use the forks to lift each half of dough into a prepared bowl. If the dough is too wet to transfer with forks, lightly grease your hands with butter or oil, then transfer each half to a bowl. Do not cover the bowls. Let the dough rise on the countertop near the oven (or another warm, draft-free spot) for 10 to 20 minutes, until the top of the dough just crowns the rims of the bowls.

4. Transfer the bowls to the oven and bake for 45 minutes, or until golden all around. Remove the bowls from the oven and turn the loaves out onto cooling racks. If the loaves look pale, return them to their bowls and bake for 5 minutes longer. Let the loaves cool for 20 minutes before cutting.

NOTE: To grate cheese quickly, pass it through your food processor using the shredder attachment.

GLUTEN-FREE PEASANT BREAD

MAKES 2 LOAVES

Gluten-free baking often feels like a science experiment, a study of unfamiliar powders, an exercise in balance—so many variables contribute to the fate of the finished product. If you do a lot of gluten-free baking, it pays to make your own mix from scratch. If you only dabble in gluten-free baking, buying a ready-made mix will save your pantry from a clutter of ingredients you may never use again. Cup4Cup, chef Thomas Keller's brand of gluten-free flour, produces a soft, light-textured crumb, strikingly similar in texture to the Peasant Bread Master Recipe (page 22), but feel free to use your favorite store-bought mix, your own blend, or the homemade blend provided at right.

4 cups (500 g) Homemade Gluten-Free Flour Blend (recipe follows) or store-bought

2 teaspoons kosher salt

2¼ teaspoons instant yeast

2 cups lukewarm water

2 tablespoons honey

2 eggs, lightly beaten

2 tablespoons neutral oil

1 teaspoon white wine or cider vinegar

Softened unsalted butter, for greasing

1. In a large bowl, whisk together the flour, salt, and instant yeast. In a medium bowl, pour the water over the honey and stir to dissolve. Add the eggs, oil, and vinegar. Add the wet ingredients to the dry and mix with a spatula to form a batter.

2. Grease two 1-quart oven-safe bowls with the softened butter—be generous. Divide the dough evenly between the prepared bowls. With wet hands, smooth the surface of the dough. Let the dough rise in a warm or draft-free spot for 30 to 45 minutes, until the top of the dough just crowns the rims of the bowls. Halfway through the rising, set a rack in the middle of the oven and preheat it to 425°F.

3. Transfer the bowls to the oven and bake for 15 minutes. Reduce the heat to 375°F and bake for 17 to 20 minutes more, until golden all around. Remove the bowls from the oven and turn the loaves out onto cooling racks. Let the loaves cool for at least 20 minutes before cutting.

Homemade Gluten-Free Flour Blend

MAKES ABOUT 8 CUPS (1.16 KG)

400 g cornstarch

200 g white rice flour

170 g brown rice flour

170 g milk powder

160 g tapioca starch

40 g potato starch

20 g xanthan gum

In a large bowl, whisk all ingredients together. Store in an airtight container at room temperature for up to 3 months.

CRANBERRY-WALNUT DINNER ROLLS

MAKES 16 TO 18 ROLLS

Studded with nuts and fruit, these rolls are festive around the holidays and especially welcome on the Thanksgiving table. Or try them sliced and set on a board beside a creamy cheese such as Camembert, Délice de Bourgogne, or Gorgonzola Dolce. For a less sweet, nut-free version, use dried apricots, which are more tart than cranberries, and sunflower seeds, which offer a nutty flavor and nice crunch. Of course, the dried fruit-and-nut combination can be varied endlessly. See Variations (page 26) for tips on adding nuts, seeds, and dried fruit.

1½ cups (170 g) walnuts

4 cups (512 g) unbleached all-purpose flour

2 teaspoons kosher salt

2 teaspoons sugar

2¼ teaspoons instant yeast

¾ cup (85 g) dried cranberries

2 cups lukewarm water

Softened unsalted butter, for greasing

1. Preheat the oven to 350°F. Lay the walnuts on a sheet pan, spreading them in a single layer. Toast in the oven for 10 minutes, or until lightly golden. Remove and transfer the walnuts to a clean tea towel and rub to remove the walnut skins. Taking care to leave as many skins behind as possible, transfer the nuts to a colander and shake to remove any remaining skins. Set aside.

2. In a large bowl, whisk together the flour, salt, sugar, and instant yeast. Add the toasted walnuts, breaking up any large pieces with your hands, and cranberries, and toss to combine. Add the water. Using a rubber spatula, mix until the liquid is absorbed and the ingredients form a sticky dough ball. Cover the bowl with a damp tea towel or plastic wrap and set aside in a warm spot to rise for 1 to 1½ hours, until the dough has doubled in bulk.

3. Set a rack in the middle of the oven and preheat it to 425°F. Grease a 12-cup muffin tin plus four to six 4-ounce ramekins or custard cups. Using two forks, deflate the dough by releasing it from the sides of the bowl and pulling it toward the center. Rotate the bowl quarter turns as you deflate, turning the mass into a rough ball.

4. Using your two forks, pull away portions of the dough and plop each into a buttered muffin cup so that dough fills it by three-quarters. Repeat until the muffin tin is filled. Scoop the remaining dough into the buttered ramekins. Let the dough rise for 10 minutes, or until it just crowns the tops of the cups.

5. Transfer the muffin tin and ramekins to the oven and bake for 10 minutes. Reduce the heat to 375°F and bake for 15 to 20 minutes more, until golden all around. Remove the rolls from the oven and turn them onto a cooling rack or directly into a bread basket.

HAMBURGER BUNS

MAKES 8 LARGE BUNS

Bring these buns to a barbecue and you will be crowned king . . . then burdened with bun duty for the rest of the summer. This is the only problem with knowing how easy it is to make hamburger buns: when the occasion calls, it's guilt inducing not to make them. A mixed seed topping—I like 1 tablespoon each of sesame, flax, poppy, and millet—looks especially striking, though a simple, more traditional sprinkling of ¼ cup sesame seeds is fine, too. If you want to shake things up, try 1 tablespoon each of poppy seeds, toasted sesame seeds, dried garlic, and dried onion—the bun tastes like an everything bagel!

4 cups (512 g) unbleached all-purpose flour, plus at least ¼ cup (32 g) for dusting

2 teaspoons kosher salt

2 teaspoons sugar

2¼ teaspoons instant yeast

2 cups lukewarm water, plus more for brushing (see Note)

Toppings of your choice (see above)

1. In a large bowl, whisk together 4 cups (512 g) flour, the salt, sugar, and instant yeast. Add 2 cups lukewarm water. Using a rubber spatula, mix until the liquid is absorbed and the ingredients form a sticky dough ball. Cover the bowl with a damp tea towel or plastic wrap and set aside in a warm spot to rise for 1 to 1½ hours, until the dough has doubled in bulk.

2. Position racks in the upper and lower thirds of the oven, and preheat it to 425°F. Line two sheet pans with parchment paper. Using two forks, deflate the dough by releasing it from the sides of the bowl and pulling it toward the center. Rotate the bowl quarter turns as you deflate, turning the mass into a rough ball.

3. Sprinkle ¼ cup (32 g) of flour onto a work surface. Using your two forks and working from the center out, separate the dough into two equal pieces. Use the forks to lift one half of the dough onto a clean surface. Using as much flour as necessary from the surface, dust your hands and the exterior of the dough, then shape the mass as best you can into a ball. Using a bench scraper or a knife, divide the mass into roughly four equal-size pieces, about the size of an apple. With floured hands, roll each portion into a ball, each about 4 inches in diameter, using the pinkie-edges of your hands to pinch the dough underneath each ball. Transfer them immediately to the prepared sheet pan. Repeat with the remaining dough, using the second sheet pan for the second half of the dough.

4. Brush the surface of each ball with water (or egg wash; see Note), flatten gently with your hand, then sprinkle with your desired toppings. Do not cover. Let the rolls rise for 20 minutes.

5. Transfer the sheet pans to the oven and bake for 15 minutes. Rotate the pans and reduce the heat to 375°F. Bake for 5 to 10 minutes more, until evenly golden. Remove the rolls from the oven, transfer them to a cooling rack, and let them cool for at least 15 minutes before slicing them crosswise.

NOTE: If you like a shiny surface on your buns, use 1 egg beaten with 1 tablespoon water to brush the tops.

BUTTERMILK PULL-APART ROLLS

MAKES 20 TO 24 (2-INCH) ROLLS

Brushed with butter and sprinkled with sea salt, this slightly sweet old-fashioned pull-apart bread resembles Parker House rolls in texture. They are festive on a holiday table but easy enough to make any night of the week. The pans filled with unbaked rolls can be stored overnight in the fridge, too.

This recipe yields about two dozen rolls, which are baked in two 8-inch pans. It sounds like a lot, but before you think about halving the recipe, consider saving one pan for dessert: halve the rolls crosswise, brush with melted butter, toast briefly, and top them with whipped cream and strawberries (see page 163).

4 cups (512 g) unbleached all-purpose flour,
   plus at least ¼ cup (32 g) for dusting

2 teaspoons kosher salt

2 tablespoons sugar

2¼ teaspoons instant yeast

1 cup boiling water

1 cup buttermilk

6 tablespoons (¾ stick) melted unsalted butter

Softened unsalted butter, for greasing

Flaky sea salt, such as fleur de sel, for sprinkling

1. In a large bowl, whisk together 4 cups (512 g) flour, the salt, sugar, and instant yeast. In a medium bowl, pour the boiling water over the buttermilk and stir to combine—the mixture will look slightly curdled. Let it cool for 10 minutes, then add it to the flour mixture. Add 4 tablespoons of the melted butter. Using a rubber spatula, mix until the liquid is absorbed and the ingredients form a sticky dough ball. Cover the bowl with a damp tea towel or plastic wrap and set it aside in a warm spot to rise for 1½ to 2 hours, until the dough has doubled in bulk.

2. Set a rack in the middle of the oven and preheat it to 375°F. Grease two 8-inch circle or square baking pans generously with the softened butter. Using two forks, deflate the dough by releasing it from the sides of the bowl and pulling it toward the center. Rotate the bowl quarter turns as you deflate, turning the mass into a rough ball.

3. Spread ¼ cup (32 g) of the flour onto a clean surface. Using your two forks and working from the center out, separate the dough into two equal pieces. Use the forks to lift one half of the dough onto your clean surface. Using as much flour as necessary from the surface, dust your hands and the exterior of the dough, then shape the mass as best you can into a ball. Using a bench scraper or a knife, divide the mass into 10 to 12 equal-size pieces, each 1- to 2-inches in diameter. Using as much flour as needed to prevent sticking, roll each piece into a ball—it's okay if each piece is a little misshapen—then transfer to one of the prepared pans, spacing them evenly apart. Repeat with the remaining dough and the second pan. Do not cover the pans. Let the dough rise on the countertop near the oven (or another warm, draft-free spot) for 20 to 25 minutes or longer (up to 1 hour if they've been refrigerated), until the dough pieces have puffed to almost fill the pans.

4. Transfer both pans to the oven and bake for 20 to 25 minutes, until golden. Remove them from the oven and immediately brush the surfaces with the remaining 2 tablespoons melted butter and sprinkle with sea salt. Let the bread cool in the pan for 5 minutes, then turn it out onto cooling racks and invert it again onto plates. Let the bread rest for 5 minutes before serving.

PISSALADIÈRE
WITH ANCHOVIES, TOMATOES, AND ONIONS

MAKES 1 (13 × 18-INCH) PISSALADIÈRE

The base of *pissaladière*, the Provençal tart topped with caramelized onions, anchovies, and olives, can be a pastry shell, a flat round of pizza dough, or even puff pastry. Here, focaccia is the base for a mix of stewed onions and fresh tomatoes, a sweet contrast to the accompanying purée of anchovies, capers, and garlic. Make this bread for an end-of-summer gathering, when the tomatoes are bountiful and the weather is hinting of fall. Present it cut into squares on your largest cutting board. It keeps well at room temperature for up to 4 hours. See the note on page 70 for instructions on how to make the dough ahead, which will create a particularly porous crumb.

for the dough

4 cups (512 g) unbleached all-purpose flour

2 teaspoons kosher salt

1 teaspoon instant yeast

2 cups lukewarm water

for assembly

6 tablespoons extra-virgin olive oil,
  plus more for greasing

3 cups sliced onions (about 3 medium onions,
  halved and thinly sliced)

Pinch of kosher salt

2 garlic cloves

4 anchovies

1 tablespoon capers

½ cup coarsely chopped pitted kalamata
  or niçoise olives

1 cup diced tomatoes

1. Make the dough: In a large bowl, whisk together the flour, salt, and instant yeast. Add the water. Using a rubber spatula, mix until the liquid is absorbed and the ingredients form a sticky dough ball. Cover the bowl with a damp tea towel or plastic wrap and set aside in a warm spot to rise for 1 to 1½ hours, until the dough has doubled in bulk.

2. Meanwhile, assemble the pissaladière: In a large sauté pan, heat 1 tablespoon olive oil over high heat. When it begins to shimmer, add the onions and a pinch of salt. Immediately reduce the heat to medium-low and cook, stirring every few minutes, until the onions are lightly golden, about 15 minutes.

3. Meanwhile, in a food processor, mince the garlic and anchovies together. Add 2 tablespoons oil and blend until smooth. Add the capers and pulse to coarsely chop. Set aside.

4. Set a rack in the middle of the oven and preheat it to 425°F. Line a rimmed sheet pan with parchment paper or coat with nonstick cooking spray. Pour the remaining 3 tablespoons oil on the sheet pan. Using two forks, deflate the dough by releasing it from the sides of the bowl and pulling it toward the center. Rotate the bowl quarter turns as you deflate, turning the mass into a rough ball. Use the forks to lift the dough onto the prepared sheet pan. Roll the dough ball in the oil to coat it all over. Let it rest without touching it for 20 minutes.

5. With lightly greased hands, press down on the dough, using all ten fingers to dimple and stretch the dough outward. Pull gently on the ends and stretch them toward the corners of the sheet pan. When the dough begins to resist being stretched, let it rest for

5 minutes, then stretch it again, continuing until it fits most of the sheet pan.

6. Spread the anchovy purée over the surface of the dough. Scatter the olives, caramelized onions, and then the tomatoes on top. Use all ten fingers again to dimple the dough and gently stretch it.

7. Transfer the sheet pan to the oven and bake for 25 to 30 minutes, until the underside is golden and crisp. Remove the pissaladière from the oven and transfer it to a cutting board. Let it cool for 10 minutes before cutting it into squares.

FOCACCIA
WITH GRAPES, PANCETTA, AND ROSEMARY

MAKES 1 (13 × 18-INCH) FOCACCIA

During the fall harvest of grapes in Tuscany, winemakers celebrate with *schiacciata con l'uva*, flatbread studded with juicy wine grapes, rosemary, and olive oil—a snack traditionally served for dessert. This variation leans more savory with the addition of pancetta, though a layer of caramelized onions creates an addictive salty-sweet dynamic. This dough takes really well to an overnight rest in the fridge, which will create a particularly porous crumb. After transferring the dough to the oiled sheet pan, let it rest for 40 minutes before stretching it.

for the dough

4 cups (512 g) unbleached all-purpose flour

2 teaspoons kosher salt

1 teaspoon instant yeast

2 cups lukewarm water

for assembly

5 tablespoons extra-virgin olive oil, plus more for greasing

3 cups sliced onions (about 3 medium onions, halved and thinly sliced)

Pinch of kosher salt

1 cup halved seedless grapes, red or green

¼ cup finely diced pancetta

1 tablespoon minced fresh rosemary

1. Make the dough: In a large bowl, whisk together the flour, salt, and instant yeast. Add the water. Using a rubber spatula, mix until the liquid is absorbed and the ingredients form a sticky dough ball. Cover the bowl with a damp tea towel or plastic wrap and set aside in a warm spot to rise for 1 to 1½ hours, until the dough has doubled in bulk.

2. Meanwhile, assemble the focaccia: In a large sauté pan, heat 1 tablespoon oil over high heat. When it begins to shimmer, add the onions and a pinch of salt. Immediately reduce the heat to medium-low and cook, stirring every few minutes, until the onions are lightly golden, about 15 minutes. Remove the pan from the heat and set aside to cool.

3. Set a rack in the middle of the oven and preheat it to 425°F. Line a rimmed sheet pan with parchment paper or coat with nonstick cooking spray. Pour 3 tablespoons of the oil on the sheet pan. Using two forks, deflate the dough by releasing it from the sides of the bowl and pulling it toward the center. Rotate the bowl quarter turns as you deflate, turning the mass into a rough ball. Use the forks to lift the dough onto the prepared sheet pan. Roll the dough ball in the oil to coat it all over. Let it rest without touching it for 20 minutes.

4. With lightly greased hands, press down on the dough, using all ten fingers to dimple and stretch the dough outward. Pull gently on the ends and stretch them toward the corners of the sheet pan. When the dough begins to resist being stretched, let it rest for 5 minutes, then stretch it again, continuing until it fits most of the sheet pan.

5. Cover the surface of the dough with the caramelized onions. Scatter the grapes, pancetta, and rosemary on top. Drizzle with the remaining tablespoon of olive oil, then use all ten fingers again to dimple the dough and gently stretch it.

6. Transfer the sheet pan to the oven and bake for 25 to 30 minutes, until golden on top and crisp on the bottom. Remove the focaccia from the oven and transfer it to a cooling rack. Let it cool for 10 minutes before cutting it into squares or strips.

NOTE: To make a focaccia for sandwiches, follow the recipe until the dough is stretched to fit the pan. Drizzle the top of the focaccia with 1 tablespoon extra-virgin olive oil, 1 teaspoon flaky sea salt, and, if desired, 1 tablespoon minced fresh rosemary. Bake for about 25 minutes or until golden brown and crisp on the bottom.

INDIVIDUAL BREAKFAST SHAKSHUKAS

SERVES 6

Shakshuka, eggs poached in a fragrant tomato sauce, originated in Tunisia, where it typically is served for breakfast or lunch with good white bread alongside for dipping. Here, the bread and *shakshuka* are combined: individual sesame-seed crusts cradle smoky tomato sauce and a runny-yolked egg, especially enjoyable for brunch or even as dinner with a light green salad.

for the dough

2 cups (255 g) unbleached all-purpose flour

1 teaspoon kosher salt

½ teaspoon instant yeast

1 cup lukewarm water

for the sauce

1 tablespoon extra-virgin olive oil

½ cup diced onion

2 garlic cloves, minced

Pinch of kosher salt

Pinch of crushed red pepper flakes

½ teaspoon cumin

½ teaspoon za'atar

1½ cups diced tomatoes (about 3 plum tomatoes)

¼ cup chopped fresh cilantro

for assembly

2 tablespoons all-purpose flour, plus more as needed

6 teaspoons extra-virgin olive oil, plus more as needed

6 teaspoons sesame seeds

6 eggs

NOTE: This dough can be prepared the night before: Keep the proportions the same but use cold water in place of lukewarm. Let it rise at room temperature for 8 to 10 hours, then proceed with the recipe as directed. The sauce can be made in advance, too, and stored in the fridge for up to a week.

1. Make the dough: In a medium bowl, whisk together the flour, salt, and instant yeast. Add the water. Using a rubber spatula, mix until the liquid is absorbed and the ingredients form a sticky dough ball. Cover the bowl with a damp tea towel or plastic wrap and set aside in a warm spot to rise for 1½ to 2 hours, until the dough has nearly doubled in bulk.

2. Meanwhile, make the sauce: In a medium sauté pan, heat the oil over medium heat. When it begins to shimmer, add the onion and sauté until soft and lightly golden, about 5 minutes. Add the garlic and cook until fragrant, 1 minute more. Sprinkle with the salt, pepper flakes, cumin, and za'atar, and stir to coat. Add the tomatoes, stir again, cover the pan, and reduce the heat to low and simmer for 5 minutes, or until the tomatoes begin to break down. Uncover the pan and cook for 5 to 10 minutes more, until the juices have evaporated and the sauce has thickened. Stir in the cilantro. Taste and adjust the seasoning with more salt or pepper flakes as needed. Remove the pan from the heat and set aside to cool.

3. Assemble the shaksukas: Position two racks in the upper and lower thirds of your oven and preheat it to 350°F. Line two sheet pans with parchment paper. Spread 2 tablespoons flour over a clean surface. Make three 1-teaspoon oil puddles on each sheet pan, evenly spacing them. Sprinkle ½ teaspoon of sesame seeds into each puddle.

4. Using two forks, deflate the dough by releasing it from the sides of the bowl and pulling it toward the center. Rotate the bowl quarter turns as you deflate, turning the mass into a rough ball.

5. Using your two forks and working from the center out, separate the dough into two equal pieces. Use the forks to lift one half of the dough onto your prepared clean surface. Use a bench scraper or knife to cut the dough into three equal pieces. With floured hands, roll each portion into a ball, using the pinkie-edges of your hands to pinch the dough underneath each ball. Place each directly on top of one prepared puddle of oil and sesame seeds and roll to coat. Repeat with the remaining dough on the second sheet pan. Let the dough sit without touching it for 20 minutes.

6. With oiled hands and working from the center out, gently stretch each dough ball into a 6- to 7-inch round. As soon as the dough begins resisting, stop stretching it, let it rest for 5 minutes, then stretch again.

7. Spoon about 2 tablespoons of sauce over each round of dough, leaving a ½-inch border, pressing down lightly in the center to create a slight cup. Brush the edges of the dough with water and sprinkle with the remaining sesame seeds.

8. Transfer the sheet pans to the oven and bake for 15 minutes, switching and rotating the sheet pans halfway through. Remove the pans from the oven and crack an egg into the center of each round. Return the pans to the oven and bake for 8 to 12 minutes more, until the egg whites are just set and the yolk is slightly runny. Serve immediately.

SOFT SANDWICH BREAD

MAKES 2 LOAVES

If you are someone who makes sandwiches often, enjoys French toast (see pages 140 and 151), or has little mouths to feed, it may make sense to make a larger quantity of the Peasant Bread Master Recipe (page 22) and to bake it in loaf pans. Adding oil to the dough keeps it soft for days, though I think you'll find a long shelf life to be irrelevant: from Toasts with Banana and Chocolate-Hazelnut Spread (page 155) at breakfast to grilled cheese sandwiches (see page 128) at lunch to vegetable strata (see page 145) for weekend brunch, this bread disappears quickly. If it offends your moral fibers to make bread without any whole-wheat flour, 1 to 2 cups of whole-wheat flour can be substituted here. Or you could make the Whole-Wheat Sandwich Bread (page 75), which uses 50 percent whole-wheat flour.

6 cups (768 g) unbleached all-purpose flour

1 tablespoon kosher salt

1 tablespoon sugar

2½ teaspoons instant yeast

3 cups lukewarm water

⅓ cup neutral oil

Softened unsalted butter, for greasing

1. In a large bowl, whisk together the flour, salt, sugar, and instant yeast. Add the water, followed by the oil. Using a rubber spatula, mix until the liquid is absorbed and the ingredients form a sticky dough ball. Cover the bowl with a damp tea towel or plastic wrap and set aside in a warm spot to rise for 1½ to 2 hours, until the dough has doubled in bulk.

2. Set a rack in the middle of the oven and preheat it to 375°F. Grease two 8.5 × 4.5-inch loaf pans generously with the softened butter. Using two forks, deflate the dough by releasing it from the sides of the bowl and pulling it toward the center. Rotate the bowl quarter turns as you deflate, turning the mass into a rough ball.

3. Using your two forks and working from the center out, separate the dough into two equal pieces. With greased hands, lift each half of dough into a prepared pan. Do not cover the pans. Let the dough rise on the countertop near the oven (or another warm, draft-free spot) for 20 to 25 minutes, until the top of the dough just crowns the rims of the pans.

4. Transfer the pans to the oven and bake for 40 to 45 minutes, until the tops are golden brown and firm to touch. Remove the pans from the oven and turn the loaves out onto a cooling rack. Let them rest on their sides for at least 15 minutes before cutting.

WHOLE-WHEAT SANDWICH BREAD

MAKES 2 LOAVES

Breads made with 100 percent whole-wheat flour tend to be dense because of the presence of bran and germ in the flour, which inhibit gluten development and hinder rising. Using 50 percent whole-wheat flour, however, will not compromise a loaf's texture. Oil increases shelf life, egg tenderizes the crumb, and honey and milk balance the slightly bitter flavor of the flour. The recipe below produces a loaf at once light and hearty, as well suited for toast as for sandwiches.

3 cups (384 g) unbleached all-purpose flour

3 cups (384 g) white whole-wheat flour (see Note)

1 tablespoon kosher salt

2½ teaspoons instant yeast

1 cup milk

1 tablespoon vinegar

½ cup boiling water

2 tablespoons honey

⅓ cup neutral oil

1 egg, lightly beaten

Softened unsalted butter, for greasing

1. In a large bowl, whisk together the flours, salt, and instant yeast. In a large bowl, combine the milk and vinegar and let sit for 5 minutes. Add the boiling water, the honey, and 1 cup water to the milk mixture and stir to dissolve. Add the wet ingredients to the flour, followed by the oil and egg. Using a rubber spatula, mix until the liquid is absorbed and the ingredients form a sticky dough ball. Cover the bowl with a damp tea towel or plastic wrap and set aside in a warm spot to rise for 1½ to 2 hours, until the dough has doubled in bulk.

2. Set a rack in the middle of the oven and preheat it to 375°F. Grease two 8.5 × 4.5-inch loaf pans generously with the softened butter. Using two forks, deflate the dough by releasing it from the sides of the bowl and pulling it toward the center. Rotate the bowl quarter turns as you deflate, turning the mass into a rough ball.

3. Using your two forks and working from the center out, separate the dough into two equal pieces. With greased hands, lift each half of dough into a prepared pan. Do not cover the pans. Let the dough rise on the countertop near the oven (or another warm, draft-free spot) for 20 to 25 minutes, until the top of the dough just crowns the rims of the pans.

4. Transfer the pans to the oven and bake for 40 to 45 minutes, until the tops are golden brown and firm to the touch. Remove the pans from the oven and turn the loaves out onto a cooling rack. Let them rest on their sides for at least 15 minutes before cutting.

NOTE: White whole-wheat flour, milled from a hard white spring or winter wheat, is lighter in color and texture than the more common red wheat. Traditional whole-wheat flour can be substituted here with equal success, yielding a slightly heavier crumb. One cup of buttermilk, too, can be used in place of the milk and vinegar.

SOUP BREAD BOWLS

MAKES 4 BOWLS

Passé shmassé—bread bowls are fun (and practical—fewer dishes to wash!). Various vessels, many of which you may have on hand, can be used to make bread bowls: a jumbo muffin tin, large custard cups, or—my favorite—empty steel-cut oat tins or coffee cans, which create flat-bottomed, sturdy, and beautifully golden bowls, perfect for cradling soup (see page 112) or presenting an array of party dips. If you are using the tins, remove the bottom with a can opener, and be careful of sharp edges while you are greasing.

4 cups (512 g) unbleached all-purpose flour

2 teaspoons kosher salt

2 teaspoons sugar

2¼ teaspoons instant yeast

2 cups lukewarm water

Softened unsalted butter, for greasing

1. In a large bowl, whisk together the flour, salt, sugar, and instant yeast. Add the water. Using a rubber spatula, mix until the liquid is absorbed and the ingredients form a sticky dough ball. Cover the bowl with a damp tea towel or plastic wrap and set aside in a warm spot to rise for 1 to 1½ hours, until the dough has doubled in bulk.

2. Set a rack in the middle of the oven and preheat it to 425°F. Grease four empty steel-cut oat tins or vessels of your choice with the softened butter and place on a greased or parchment-lined sheet pan. Using two forks, deflate the dough by releasing it from the sides of the bowl and pulling it toward the center. Rotate the bowl quarter turns as you deflate, turning the mass into a rough ball.

3. Using your two forks and working from the center out, separate the dough into two equal pieces. Using the forks, divide each half in half. Use the forks to lift each portion of dough into a prepared vessel—be careful not to move them once the dough is plopped inside because it will creep out the sides. Let the dough rise for 20 minutes or until doubled—the dough will not crown the rims of the tins.

4. Transfer the sheet pan with the tins to the oven and bake for 15 minutes. Reduce the heat to 375°F and bake for 10 to 15 minutes more, until golden. Remove the sheet pan from the oven and turn the breads out onto a cooling rack. Let them cool completely, at least 1 hour, before creating the bread bowl.

5. To make the bread bowl, use a small serrated knife to carve a circle out of the top of each loaf; set aside. Use your hand to scoop out the bread, leaving a ½-inch border all the way around. Save this bread for croutons (see page 182), crumbs (see page 172), or for eating with the soup.

6. Preheat the oven to 375°F. Place the hollowed-out bowls back onto the parchment-lined sheet pan, along with their tops. Transfer the pan to the oven and bake for 15 minutes. Remove the pan from the oven and transfer the bread bowls to plates or shallow bowls. Ladle in piping hot soup and serve the bread bowls immediately.

PEASANT PIZZA

SERVES 2 TO 4

This pizza is thin and sturdy, ideal for little hands (and palates), but crisp and delicious enough to entice the pickiest of pizza connoisseurs who are forever after that pliable, ballooned, and blistered Neopolitan crust. For the best results, handle the dough delicately and bake it on a preheated Baking Steel, a ¼-inch thick slab of steel that creates crisp bottom crusts and airy edges, or a pizza stone in a screaming hot oven, though an upside-down rimmed sheet pan can be used instead. You can also try it in a skillet—cast-iron gives excellent results (see alternate recipe, page 80). Inspired by *tarte flambée*, a specialty of the French region Alsace, the toppings here are geared more for adults. To make the seasonal variations, scatter the toppings lightly over the crème fraîche, and follow with the onion, thyme (if using), bacon, and grated cheese. When I make this for my children, I use store-bought tomato sauce and pregrated mozzarella—the horror!—and they gobble it up.

for the dough

2 cups (255 g) unbleached all-purpose flour

1 teaspoon kosher salt

½ teaspoon instant yeast

1 cup lukewarm water

for assembly

¼ cup (32 g) all-purpose flour, plus more for dusting

6 to 9 tablespoons crème fraîche

¾ to 1½ cups thinly sliced onion

1½ teaspoons finely minced thyme (optional)

3 slices uncooked or cooked bacon, finely minced

¾ cup grated Gruyère

Extra-virgin olive oil

Sea salt

seasonal toppings (optional)

Spring: paper-thin slices of raw potatoes

Summer: sliced peach and ricotta

Fall: blanched butternut squash slices and sage

Winter: sautéed pear and blue cheese

1. Make the dough (see Note, page 80): In a medium bowl, whisk together the flour, salt, and instant yeast. Add the water. Using a rubber spatula, mix until the liquid is absorbed and the ingredients form a sticky dough ball. Cover the bowl with a damp tea towel or plastic wrap and set aside in a warm spot to rise for 1½ hours, or until the dough has nearly doubled in bulk.

2. Place a Baking Steel or pizza stone on a rack positioned in the upper third of the oven and preheat it to 550°F for at least 45 minutes. Using two forks, deflate the dough by releasing it from the sides of the bowl and pulling it toward the center. Rotate the bowl quarter turns as you deflate, turning the mass into a rough ball.

3. Assemble the pizza: Using your two forks, divide the dough into three equal portions; the portions will look small. Spread ¼ cup flour onto a clean surface. Use the forks to lift each portion of the dough onto the surface. With floured hands, roll each portion into a ball, using the pinkie-edges of your hands to pinch the dough underneath each ball.

(recipe continues)

Let the balls sit on their tucked-in edges for at least 20 minutes without touching.

4. Place a sheet of parchment paper on a pizza peel. With floured hands, pick up one round of dough and gently stretch it outward—you want to preserve all of the pockets of air trapped in the dough. Then, with the backs of your hands, stretch the round more, using additional flour as needed. As soon as the dough hints at tearing, lay it on the parchment-lined peel. Stretch more if necessary—the round should be 8 to 10 inches in diameter.

5. Drop 2 to 3 tablespoons of the crème fraîche evenly around the dough, and spread it around lightly using the back of a spoon. If you are making a seasonal variation, add the specified toppings. Scatter ¼ to ½ cup onion, ½ teaspoon thyme (if using), 1 slice minced bacon, and ¼ cup grated cheese over the top. Drizzle lightly with olive oil. Season with a pinch of salt.

6. Shimmy the round of dough, parchment paper and all, onto the heated Baking Steel or pizza stone. Bake for 5 minutes or until the edges are golden. Use the peel to remove the pizza from the oven, transfer it to a cutting board, and repeat with the remaining dough. You can assemble the remaining rounds of dough on separate sheets of parchment paper while the first pizza bakes.

NOTE: The dough can be mixed first thing in the morning and left to rise all day on the counter—be sure to wrap the bowl tightly in plastic wrap to prevent the dough from drying out. Or it can be prepared 3 hours before dinnertime.

Skillet Peasant Pizza

SERVES 2 TO 4

1. Follow the Peasant Pizza recipe through step 3. Set a rack in the center of the oven and preheat it to 550°F. Drizzle ½ teaspoon extra-virgin olive oil into each of three 8- to 10-inch oven-safe skillets. Transfer one ball of dough to each skillet, and roll in the oil to coat.

2. With oiled hands and working from the center out, gently stretch the dough to fit the skillet. As soon as the dough begins resisting or tearing, stop, let it rest for 5 minutes, then stretch again—small tears are fine and can easily be pinched back together.

3. Top the pizzas as directed in the Peasant Pizza recipe, then place the skillets in the oven, one or two at a time, and bake for 8 to 10 minutes, until the pizza's edges are golden. Check the underside with a metal spatula; it should be crisp and golden-brown. If the underside of the crust is still pale, continue baking for 3 to 5 minutes, or place the pan over a burner on medium-high heat for about a minute, keeping an eye on it the entire time and continuing to peek at the underside.

SAVORY MONKEY BREAD
WITH GRUYÈRE, SCALLIONS, AND BACON

SERVES 8 TO 10 AS AN APPETIZER

My dear friend Shannon Buth passed along this recipe, a festive savory monkey bread her mother, Linda Christ, whom I was not so fortunate to meet, made for every gathering she hosted. Baked in a Dutch oven or Bundt pan, this bread rises dramatically, emerging with a golden layer of cheese enshrouding a tangle of poppy-seed-specked puffs. It is a crowd-pleaser through and through and, as Shannon promised, disappears about as quickly as it is turned out. Serve it to a crowd of rowdy sports fans, who will ooh and aah as they attack it, each pull revealing bits of scallions and bacon caught in the buttery crevices.

for the dough

4 cups (512 g) unbleached all-purpose flour

2 teaspoons kosher salt

2 teaspoons sugar

2¼ teaspoons instant yeast

2 cups lukewarm water

for assembly

6 slices bacon, finely chopped

8 tablespoons (1 stick) butter, softened, plus more for greasing

1 tablespoon Dijon mustard

1 tablespoon poppy seeds

1 cup grated Gruyère cheese

1 cup grated mozzarella cheese

¼ cup (32 g) unbleached all-purpose flour, plus more as needed

½ cup thinly sliced scallions, white and green parts

NOTE: Monkey bread can be assembled ahead and stored in fridge. After the final layer of cheese is scattered on top, cover the pan with plastic wrap and place in fridge for as long as 12 hours. When ready to bake, remove from fridge as oven preheats. Proceed with step 6.

(recipe continues)

1. Make the dough: In a large bowl, whisk together the flour, salt, sugar, and instant yeast. Add the water. Using a rubber spatula, mix until the liquid is absorbed and the ingredients form a sticky dough ball. Cover the bowl with a damp tea towel or plastic wrap and set aside in a warm spot to rise for 1 to 1½ hours, until the dough has doubled in bulk.

2. Meanwhile, assemble the monkey bread: In a small skillet over medium-low heat, cook the bacon until crisp and its fat is rendered. Remove to a paper-towel-lined plate to drain. In a small bowl, mix 8 tablespoons butter with the mustard and poppy seeds until combined. In another small bowl, combine the cheeses. Set aside.

3. Set a rack in the middle of the oven and preheat it to 350°F. Grease a 3-quart Dutch oven or Bundt pan with softened butter. Spread ¼ cup (32 g) flour over a clean surface. Using two forks, deflate the dough by releasing it from the sides of the bowl and pulling it toward the center. Rotate the bowl quarter turns as you deflate, turning the mass into a rough ball.

4. Using your two forks and working from the center out, separate the dough into two equal pieces. Use the forks to lift one half of the dough onto the prepared surface. Using as much flour as necessary from the surface, dust your hands and the exterior of the dough, then shape the mass as best you can into a ball. Using a bench scraper or a knife, divide the mass into twelve to fourteen equal-size pieces, each a little larger than a golf ball. Using as much flour as needed to prevent sticking, shape each piece into a rough ball—no need to make these perfect—and immediately transfer them to the greased pan until you've filled the bottom.

5. Top the layer of dough balls with half the butter mixture, half the bacon, half the scallions, and half the cheese. Add more flour to your clean surface if necessary, then portion the remaining dough in same manner, transferring it to the pan to create a second layer. Top with the remaining butter mixture, bacon, scallions, and cheese. Let the dough rise in a warm spot for 20 to 25 minutes, until slightly puffed (see Note, page 81).

6. Transfer the pan to the oven and bake for 35 to 40 minutes, until golden. Remove the monkey bread from the oven, let it cool for 5 minutes, then invert it onto a large plate or cutting board. Serve the monkey bread immediately.

BRIOCHE
WITH HAZELNUT CREAM SWIRL

MAKES 2 LOAVES

Swirled with hazelnut cream, a buttery spread made in the same fashion as Frangipane (page 150), this rich brioche is nearly a meal in itself—albeit a very sweet one! Slice it thickly, spread it with the lightest dab of butter, and serve it for breakfast or afternoon tea. Do note that this recipe breaks all of the Peasant Bread tenets, requiring you to use your hands and dirty your countertops, but it illustrates how a simple dough can be adapted to more intricate applications. For an even richer variation, sprinkle the hazelnut cream with a handful of chopped toasted walnuts and diced dried figs.

for the hazelnut cream

1 cup hazelnuts

½ cup confectioners' sugar

¼ teaspoon kosher salt

8 tablespoons (1 stick) unsalted butter, softened

1 teaspoon vanilla extract

1 egg

for the dough

6 cups (768 g) unbleached all-purpose flour

1 tablespoon kosher salt

⅓ cup (77 g) sugar

2½ teaspoons instant yeast

6 tablespoons (¾ stick) unsalted butter, melted

2 cups lukewarm water

½ cup 2 percent or whole milk

2 eggs

for assembly

¼ to ½ cup (32 to 64 g) flour, for dusting

Softened unsalted butter, for greasing

1 egg mixed with 1 tablespoon water, for egg wash

1. Make the hazelnut cream: Preheat the oven to 350°F. Lay the hazelnuts on a sheet pan, spreading in a single layer. Toast in the oven for 12 minutes, or until lightly golden. Remove and transfer the hazelnuts to a clean tea towel and rub to remove the skins. Let the nuts cool completely, transfer them to a food processor, pulsing until they liquefy, about 6 minutes. Scrape down the sides of the machine, then add the confectioners' sugar, salt, butter, and vanilla. Pulse again to combine. Add the egg and blend until emulsified. Transfer the hazelnut cream to a glass jar and store it in the fridge for up to 2 weeks.

2. Make the dough: In a large bowl, whisk together the flour, salt, sugar, and instant yeast. In a separate large bowl combine the melted butter, water, and milk. Add the eggs and whisk to combine. Pour the wet ingredients into the dry and mix with a rubber spatula until combined—the mixture will be wet and sticky. Cover the bowl with a tea towel or plastic wrap and let the dough rise in a warm spot for 1½ to 2 hours, until doubled in bulk.

3. Assemble the brioche: When the dough has risen, sprinkle ¼ cup (32 g) of flour onto a clean surface. Using two forks, deflate the dough by releasing it from the sides of the bowl and pulling it toward the center. Rotate the bowl quarter turns as you deflate, turning the mass into a rough ball.

(recipe continues)

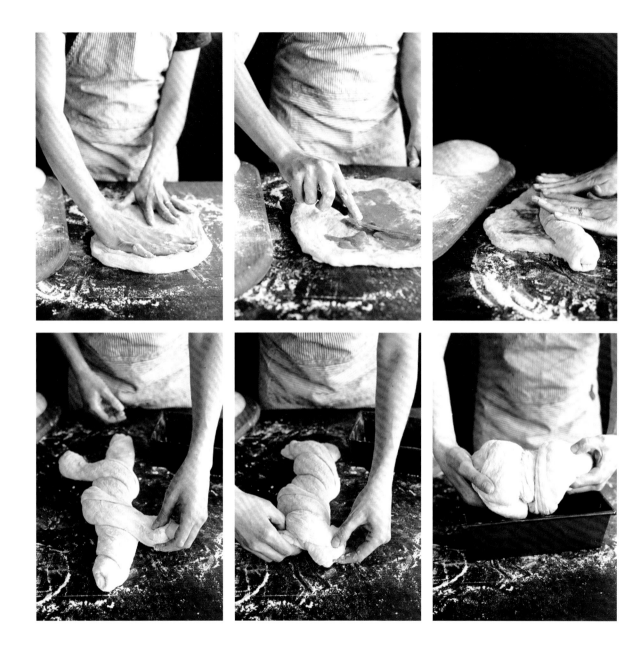

4. Using your two forks and working from the center out, separate the dough into two equal pieces. Use the forks to lift one portion of dough onto a clean surface. Cut the portion in half again, and, using as much flour as necessary from the board, shape the mass as best you can into a ball. Repeat with the remaining portion of dough to create four equal-size balls, each about 6 inches in diameter. Let the dough balls rest for 20 minutes without touching them.

5. Set a rack in the middle of the oven and preheat it to 375°F. Grease two 8.5 × 4.5-inch or 9 × 5-inch loaf pans generously with the softened butter and set aside. Dust another clean surface with 2 tablespoons flour. Transfer one dough ball to the prepared surface and, gently using your hands, stretch it from the center out into an 8 × 11-inch oval or rectangle—it doesn't have to be perfect. Spread one-quarter of the hazelnut cream on top. Starting from one short end of the oval/rectangle, roll the dough tightly into a coil. Repeat with one more round. Lay one rolled coil over the other rolled coil to make a plus sign. Twist the ends around each other to create a spiral. Transfer the spiral to a greased loaf pan. Repeat the above process with the remaining two dough balls. Brush the top of the coiled dough with the egg wash. Do not cover the pans.

6. Let the dough rise on the countertop near the oven (or another warm, draft-free spot) for 10 to 15 minutes, until it puffs above the rims.

7. Transfer the pans to the oven and bake for 45 minutes until the tops are golden brown and firm to the touch. Remove the pans from the oven and turn the loaves out onto a cooling rack. Let them cool on their sides for 20 minutes before cutting them.

PUMPKIN HARVEST BREAD

Sweetened with dates and honey, mottled with nuts and seeds, this bread is especially festive during the fall. Though the pumpkin tints the crumb orange, its overall flavor is muted, defying pumpkin naysayers and lending both softness and chew. In combination with the rich hue, the specks of pecans, seeds, and dates make for especially pretty and tasty melba toasts (see page 107).

¼ cup (40 g) raw pumpkin seeds

¼ cup (40 g) raw sunflower seeds

¼ cup (29 g) raw, unsalted roughly chopped pecans

1 cup canned unsweetened pumpkin

¼ cup honey

1½ cups boiling water

4 cups (512 g) unbleached all-purpose flour

2 teaspoons kosher salt

2¼ teaspoons instant yeast

8 or 9 pitted Medjool dates, chopped in ¼-inch pieces (about ¾ cup)

Softened unsalted butter, for greasing

1. In a large skillet over medium heat, toast the pumpkin and sunflower seeds and the pecans, stirring, for 5 to 7 minutes, until beginning to turn golden. Transfer to a plate to cool.

2. In a medium bowl, combine the pumpkin, honey, and boiling water. Stir until smooth. Set aside until lukewarm, about 20 minutes.

3. In a large bowl, whisk together the flour, salt, and instant yeast. Add the cooled seeds and pecans as well as the chopped dates and toss to combine. Pour in the pumpkin mixture and stir with a spatula to combine the ingredients into a sticky dough ball. Cover the bowl with a damp tea towel or plastic wrap and set aside in a warm spot to rise for 1½ to 2 hours, until the dough has doubled in bulk.

4. Set a rack in the middle of the oven and preheat it to 375°F. Grease two 1-quart oven-safe bowls with the softened butter—be generous. Using two forks, deflate the dough by releasing it from the sides of the bowl and pulling it toward the center. Rotate the bowl quarter turns as you deflate, turning the mass into a rough ball.

5. Using your two forks and working from the center out, separate the dough into two equal pieces. Use the forks to lift each half of dough into a prepared bowl. If the dough is too wet to transfer with forks, lightly grease your hands with butter or oil, then transfer each half to a bowl. Do not cover the bowls. Let the dough rise on the countertop near the oven (or another warm, draft-free spot) for 20 to 25 minutes, until the dough begins to crown the rims of the bowls.

6. Transfer the bowls to the oven and bake for 35 to 40 minutes, until golden all around. Remove the bowls from the oven and turn the loaves out onto cooling racks. If the loaves look pale, return them to their bowls and bake for 5 minutes longer. Let the loaves cool for 20 minutes before cutting them.

CHOCOLATE-STUDDED PANETTONE

MAKES 1 (1-POUND) PANETTONE; SERVES 10 TO 12

Around the holidays, it's nearly impossible to walk by an Italian market and not feel lured by the loaves of panettone bundled in cellophane and tied with bows, like presents begging for a home. Panettone is almost a cross between a cake and a bread, and while it couldn't be more beautiful, I've never loved the traditional flavorings: citrusy, floral extracts and candied fruit. But when these seasonings are replaced with vanilla and chunks of chocolate, which suspend in the buttery crumb, well, this is a panettone I can get behind: a treat freshly baked, and even better one day later, toasted, spread with butter, and sprinkled with sea salt.

4 cups (512 g) unbleached all-purpose flour

2 teaspoons kosher salt

¼ cup (55 g) sugar

2½ teaspoons instant yeast

1½ cups 2 percent or whole milk

½ cup boiling water

5 tablespoons unsalted butter, melted

1 teaspoon vanilla extract

Softened unsalted butter, for greasing

6 ounces (170 g) bittersweet chocolate, 60% to 70% cacao, coarsely chopped into ¼- to ½-inch pieces

1. In a large bowl, whisk together the flour, salt, sugar, and instant yeast. In a medium bowl, combine the milk, water, 4 tablespoons melted butter, and vanilla. Stir to combine, then add to the flour. Using a rubber spatula, mix until the liquid is absorbed and the ingredients form a sticky dough ball. Cover the bowl with a damp tea towel or plastic wrap and set aside in a warm spot to rise for 1½ to 2 hours, until the dough has doubled in bulk.

2. Set a rack in the middle of the oven and preheat it to 375°F. Grease a panettone mold (see Note) with the softened butter—be generous. Sprinkle the chocolate pieces over the surface of the dough. Using two forks, deflate the dough by releasing it from the sides of the bowl and pulling it toward the center. Rotate the bowl quarter turns as you deflate, turning the mass into a rough ball. Keep turning the dough in this manner until the chocolate is incorporated.

3. Use your two forks to transfer the dough to the prepared mold. If the dough is too wet to transfer with forks, lightly grease your hands with butter or oil, then transfer it to the mold. Do not cover the mold. Let the dough rise on the countertop near the oven (or another warm, draft-free spot) for 20 to 25 minutes, until the dough has doubled in bulk—it may not crown the rim, but it will come close.

4. Set the mold on a sheet pan and transfer it to the oven. Bake the mold for 40 to 45 minutes, or until uniformly brown. Remove the pan and mold from the oven and set the mold onto a cooling rack. Brush the top with the remaining tablespoon melted butter. Let the panettone cool for at least 1 hour before cutting it.

NOTE: Find panettone molds in specialty stores and online, or make your own: Use a 6- to 7-inch round baking dish. Stand a piece of parchment paper vertically along the inside edge so that it extends past the height of the pan at least 5 inches. Cut as needed and use a stapler to secure multiple sheets. Use nonstick cooking spray instead of butter. Or you can divide the dough in half and bake it in two 1-quart Pyrex bowls.

LIGHT BRIOCHE

MAKES 2 LOAVES

With heaps of butter, eggs, milk, and sugar, brioche promises big rewards. Often it delivers, but if you're the sort who views brioche more as a vehicle for what's to come—à la custard soaks and butter baths—it may not be the best use of all those costly pantry items. Lighter versions like this one, made with a fraction of the enrichments, are perfectly satisfying on their own and ideal for many a days-old resurrection: French toast (see pages 140 and 151), bread pudding (see page 236), Apple Charlotte (page 160), summer pudding (see page 159), and broiled frangipane toasts (see page 150), to name a few.

6 cups (768 g) unbleached all-purpose flour

1 tablespoon kosher salt

⅓ cup (77 g) sugar

2½ teaspoons instant yeast

6 tablespoons (¾ stick) unsalted butter, melted

2 cups lukewarm water

½ cup 2 percent or whole milk

2 eggs, lightly beaten

Softened unsalted butter, for greasing

1. In a large bowl, whisk together the flour, salt, sugar, and instant yeast. In a separate large bowl combine the melted butter, water, and milk. Add the eggs and whisk to combine. Pour the liquid ingredients into the dry and mix with a rubber spatula until combined; the mixture will be wet and sticky. Cover the bowl with a tea towel or plastic wrap and let the dough rise in a warm spot for 1½ to 2 hours, until doubled in bulk.

2. Set a rack in the middle of the oven and preheat it to 375°F. Grease two 8.5 × 4.5-inch loaf pans generously with the softened butter. Using two forks, deflate the dough by releasing it from the sides of the bowl and pulling it toward the center. Rotate the bowl quarter turns as you deflate, turning the mass into a rough ball.

3. Using the two forks and working from the center out, separate the dough into two equal pieces. Lightly grease your hands with butter or oil, and use your hands to lift each half of dough into a prepared pan. Do not cover the pans. Let the dough rise on the countertop near the oven (or another warm, draft-free spot) for about 20 minutes, or until the top of the dough just crowns the rims of the pans.

4. Transfer the pans to the oven and bake for 40 to 45 minutes, until the tops are golden brown and firm to the touch. Remove the pans from the oven and turn the loaves out onto a cooling rack. Let them cool resting on their sides for 15 minutes before cutting them.

TOASTED COCONUT LOAF

MAKES 2 LOAVES

Coconut milk, coconut oil, and shredded coconut combine in this fragrant, slightly sweet loaf. Serve it warm or toasted with butter, homemade chocolate-hazelnut spread (see page 155), or lime curd. Unsweetened shredded coconut is preferable here for its subtle, pure flavor.

1 heaping cup (56 g) unsweetened shredded coconut

4 cups (512 g) unbleached all-purpose flour

2 teaspoons kosher salt

¼ cup (55 g) sugar

2½ teaspoons instant yeast

1 cup unsweetened well-stirred coconut milk

1 cup boiling water

¼ cup melted coconut oil

Softened unsalted butter, for greasing

1. In a large sauté pan set over medium heat, lightly toast the shredded coconut, stirring frequently with a wooden spoon until it begins to turn golden, 5 to 7 minutes. Transfer to a plate to cool, about 5 minutes.

2. In a large bowl, whisk together the flour, salt, sugar, and instant yeast. Add the toasted coconut and toss to coat. In a separate large bowl, whisk together the coconut milk and boiling water. Add the mixture to the flour, followed by the oil. Using a rubber spatula, mix until the liquid is absorbed and the ingredients form a sticky dough ball. Cover the bowl with a damp tea towel or plastic wrap and set aside in a warm spot to rise for 1½ to 2 hours, until the dough has doubled in bulk.

3. Set a rack in the middle of the oven and preheat it to 375°F. Grease two 1-quart oven-safe bowls with the softened butter—be generous. Using two forks, deflate the dough by releasing it from the sides of the bowl and pulling it toward the center. Rotate the bowl quarter turns as you deflate, turning the mass into a rough ball.

4. Using your two forks and working from the center out, separate the dough into two equal pieces. Use the forks to lift each half of dough into a prepared bowl. If the dough is too wet to transfer with forks, lightly grease your hands with butter or oil, then transfer each half to a bowl. Do not cover the bowls. Let the dough rise on the countertop near the oven (or another warm, draft-free spot) for 15 to 25 minutes, until the top of the dough just crowns the rims of the bowls.

5. Transfer the bowls to the oven and bake for 35 to 40 minutes, until golden all around. Remove the bowls from the oven and turn the loaves out onto cooling racks. If the loaves look pale, return them to their bowls and bake 5 minutes longer. Let the loaves cool for 15 minutes before cutting them.

CINNAMON-SUGAR MONKEY BREAD

SERVES 4

The key to making monkey bread, sweet or savory, is to handle the dough as minimally as possible. Don't get hung up on forming perfect balls—irregularity is part of the charm of this communal breakfast or dessert. As the portions of dough rise, their imperfections dissolve into a cobble of cinnamon-sugar-encrusted puffs. The glaze is optional, though a drizzle just before the mass is pulled to pieces makes for a pretty presentation.

2 cups (255 g) unbleached all-purpose flour, plus ¼ cup (32 g) for dusting

1 teaspoon kosher salt

1 teaspoon plus ¼ cup (55 g) granulated sugar

1 teaspoon instant yeast

1 cup lukewarm water

Softened unsalted butter, for greasing

1 teaspoon cinnamon

4 tablespoons (½ stick) unsalted butter, melted

½ cup confectioners' sugar

2 teaspoons milk, plus more as needed

1. In a medium bowl, whisk together 2 cups flour, salt, 1 teaspoon granulated sugar, and instant yeast. Add the water. Using a rubber spatula, mix until the liquid is absorbed and the ingredients form a sticky dough ball. Cover the bowl with a damp tea towel or plastic wrap and set aside in a warm spot to rise for 1 to 1½ hours, until the dough has doubled in bulk.

2. Set a rack in the middle of the oven and preheat it to 375°F. Grease an 8- or 9-inch cast-iron skillet or circular or square baking pan with the softened butter. In a small bowl, stir together the cinnamon and remaining ¼ cup granulated sugar. Sprinkle 1 tablespoon of the mixture over the bottom of the prepared skillet.

3. Spread ¼ cup flour over a clean surface. Using two forks, deflate the dough by releasing it from the sides of the bowl and pulling it toward the center. Rotate the bowl quarter turns as you deflate, turning the mass into a rough ball. Use the forks to lift the dough onto the prepared clean surface. Using as much flour as necessary from the surface, dust your hands and the exterior of the dough, then shape the mass as best you can into a ball. Using a bench scraper or a knife, divide the mass into twelve to fourteen equal-size pieces, each 1 to 2 inches in diameter. Using as much flour as needed to prevent sticking, shape each piece into a rough ball and immediately transfer them to the greased pan, evenly spaced. Let rise for 20 to 25 minutes. The balls may not rise to fill the skillet entirely, but they will puff when they bake.

4. Brush each ball with some melted butter, then pour over the remainder. Sprinkle with the remaining cinnamon-sugar mixture. Transfer the skillet to the oven and bake for 20 to 25 minutes, until golden.

5. Meanwhile, make the glaze: Whisk together the confectioners' sugar and milk in a small bowl until it reaches a pourable consistency, adding more milk as needed. Remove the monkey bread from the oven and let it cool for 5 minutes in pan before inverting pan onto plate, then invert it again onto serving platter. Drizzle with glaze. Serve immediately.

DARK CHOCOLATE BREAD

MAKES 2 LOAVES

In baked goods, coffee and chocolate are often paired together; though the taste of the coffee is indiscernible, it intensifies the chocolate flavor. Here, cocoa, chopped bittersweet chocolate, and coffee combine into a rich, dense loaf that gets better by the day. This bread requires a longer rise than most other loaves here because of the high amount of sugar, and it benefits from a long cooling, too, so plan ahead. Serve it warm or toasted with butter, or spread it with mascarpone and sugared strawberries (see page 153).

3⅓ cups (432 g) unbleached all-purpose flour

¾ cup plus 2 tablespoons (70 g) unsweetened cocoa, such as Hershey's Natural

2 teaspoons kosher salt

¾ cup (170 g) sugar

2½ teaspoons instant yeast

4 ounces (113 g) bittersweet chocolate, 60% cacao, such as Ghirardelli, cut into ¼- to ½-inch pieces

½ cup hot coffee

Softened unsalted butter, for greasing

1. In a large bowl, whisk together the flour, cocoa, salt, sugar, and instant yeast. Add the chocolate pieces and toss to coat. In a small bowl, combine the coffee with 1½ cups water. Pour the wet ingredients into the dry, and using a rubber spatula, mix until the liquid is absorbed and the ingredients form a sticky dough ball—the batter will be dense. Cover the bowl with a damp tea towel or plastic wrap and set aside in a warm spot to rise for about 2 hours, or until the dough has doubled in bulk.

2. Set a rack in the middle of the oven and preheat it to 350°F. Grease two 1-quart oven-safe bowls with the softened butter—be generous. Using two forks, deflate the dough by releasing it from the sides of the bowl and pulling it toward the center. Rotate the bowl quarter turns as you deflate, turning the mass into a rough ball.

3. Using your two forks and working from the center out, separate the dough into two equal pieces. Use the forks to lift each half of dough into a prepared bowl. If the dough is too wet to transfer with forks, lightly grease your hands with butter or oil, then transfer each half to a bowl. Do not cover the bowls. Let the dough rise on the countertop near the oven (or another warm, draft-free spot) for 15 to 25 minutes until the top of the dough just crowns the rims of the bowls.

4. Transfer the bowls to the oven and bake for 45 minutes or until the surface is beginning to crisp. Remove the bowls from the oven and turn the loaves out onto cooling racks. If the loaves feel soft, return them to their bowls and bake for 5 minutes longer. Let the loaves cool for at least 30 minutes before cutting them.

EARL GREY TEA BREAD

MAKES 2 LOAVES

Bergamot, the variety of orange used to flavor Earl Grey tea, has a bold, herbal flavor with a hint of citrus. This distinct essence can be infused in baked goods by grinding the tea leaves to a fine powder, or by steeping the leaves in liquid, as here. For a stronger Earl Grey taste, use 3 tea bags or 3 teaspoons of loose tea—and if you are using loose tea, be sure to strain it after steeping. This aromatic loaf makes great breakfast toast but is especially good with your best afternoon cuppa.

1¼ cups 2 percent or whole milk

2 Earl Grey tea bags (such as Twinings) or
  2 teaspoons crushed Earl Grey tea leaves (see Note)

¼ cup honey

½ cup cold water

¼ cup neutral oil

4 cups (512 g) unbleached all-purpose flour

2 teaspoons kosher salt

2¼ teaspoons instant yeast

Zest of 1 orange (about 1 teaspoon)

Softened unsalted butter, for greasing

1. In a small pot, combine the milk and the tea bags, and bring to a boil over high heat, watching closely so it doesn't boil over. When it just comes to a boil, transfer the milk with the tea bags to a medium bowl and steep for 10 minutes, then remove the bags, squeezing out any excess liquid. Stir in the honey to dissolve, followed by the water and oil.

2. Meanwhile, in a large bowl, whisk together the flour, salt, instant yeast, and zest. Pour the liquid mixture into the flour. Using a rubber spatula, stir until the liquid is absorbed and the ingredients form a sticky dough ball. Cover the bowl with a damp tea towel or plastic wrap and set aside in a warm spot to rise for 1½ to 2 hours, until the dough has doubled in bulk.

3. Set a rack in the middle of the oven and preheat it to 375°F. Grease two 1-quart oven-safe bowls with the softened butter—be generous. Using two forks, deflate the dough by releasing it from the sides of the bowl and pulling it toward the center. Rotate the bowl quarter turns as you deflate, turning the mass into a rough ball.

4. Using your two forks and working from the center out, separate the dough into two equal pieces. Use the forks to lift each half of dough into a prepared bowl. If the dough is too wet to transfer with forks, lightly grease your hands with butter or oil, then transfer each half to a bowl. Do not cover the bowls. Let the dough rise on the countertop near the oven (or another warm, draft-free spot) for 15 to 25 minutes, until the top of the dough just crowns the rims of the bowls.

5. Transfer the bowls to the oven and bake for 35 to 40 minutes, until golden all around. Remove the bowls from the oven and turn the loaves out onto cooling racks. If the loaves look pale, return them to their bowls and bake for 5 minutes longer. Let the loaves cool for 15 minutes before cutting them.

NOTE: For a simple variation, substitute the Earl Grey tea with 1 teaspoon of culinary lavender, crushed with a mortar and pestle or ground fine in a grinder. Whisk it together with the flour, salt, and instant yeast.

CINNAMON-SWIRL BREAD

MAKES 2 LOAVES

Nearly every morning for breakfast, I slather toast with butter, shower cinnamon and sugar over the top, and present the slices to the little ones surrounding my kitchen table. Nothing, however, beats the real thing: a tender, fragrant loaf, swirled with cinnamon and sugar. The key here is to allow the dough to rest for 20 minutes after deflating and portioning it, which relaxes the gluten, enabling it to stretch easily, therefore precluding the need for a rolling pin.

for the dough

6 cups (768 g) unbleached all-purpose flour

1 tablespoon kosher salt

¼ cup (55 g) sugar

2½ teaspoons instant yeast

1½ cups buttermilk or milk

1 cup boiling water

6 tablespoons (¾ stick) unsalted butter, melted

Softened unsalted butter, for greasing

for assembly

¼ cup (32 g) flour, for clean surface

½ cup (110 g) sugar

1 tablespoon cinnamon

1 egg beaten with 1 teaspoon water

1. Make the dough: In a large bowl, whisk together the flour, salt, sugar, and instant yeast. In a medium bowl, combine the buttermilk, the boiling water, and ½ cup water. Stir to combine, then add to the flour mixture, followed by the melted butter. Mix until the liquid is absorbed and the ingredients form a sticky dough ball. Cover the bowl with a damp tea towel or plastic wrap and set aside in a warm spot to rise for 1½ hours, or until the dough has doubled in bulk.

2. Set a rack in the middle of the oven and preheat it to 375°F. Grease two 8.5 × 4.5-inch loaf pans generously with the softened butter. Using two forks, deflate the dough by releasing it from the sides of the bowl and pulling it toward the center. Rotate the bowl quarter turns as you deflate, turning the mass into a rough ball.

3. Assemble the bread: Sprinkle the flour onto a clean surface. Using your two forks and working from the center out, separate the dough into two equal pieces. Use the forks to lift one portion of dough onto the clean surface. Using as much flour as necessary from the surface, dust your hands and the exterior of the dough, and shape the mass as best you can into a ball. Repeat with the other half. Let the dough balls rest for 20 minutes without touching.

4. Dust another clean surface with flour. Transfer one round to the prepared surface and gently stretch the dough into roughly a 10 × 15-inch rectangle. In a small bowl, mix the sugar with the cinnamon. Brush the dough with the egg wash. Sprinkle the dough with half of the cinnamon-sugar mix. Beginning with one short end, roll it tightly into a coil and place it in a greased loaf pan. Repeat with the remaining round. Do not cover the pans. Let the coils rise on the countertop near the oven (or another warm, draft-free spot) for about 10 minutes, or until the top of the dough just crowns the rims of the pans.

5. Transfer the pans to the oven and bake for 40 to 45 minutes, until the tops are golden brown and firm to the touch. Remove the loaves from the oven, turn them out onto a cooling rack, and let them cool on their sides for 20 minutes before cutting them.

NOTE: To make cinnamon raisin bread, plump 1 cup of raisins in just enough water or rum to cover for 10 minutes. Drain and add them to the flour bowl after whisking the flour, salt, sugar, and yeast together. Toss to coat, and proceed as instructed.

TOAST

In its purest form, toast is a superlative vehicle for everything from pats of butter sprinkled with sea salt to mashed avocado squeezed with lemon to poached eggs peppered generously. But as you will quickly see, this section is not filled strictly with toast-as-we-know-it recipes. Rather it's a reflection of phase two of bread's life cycle, when bread begins showing its age, a softened crust, a drier crumb. If this second phase can be viewed as a spectrum, on one end you'll find sandwiches, made with the freshest bread, soft slices melding into various fillings; on the other, you'll find French toast and strata, made with days-old bread soaked in custard. In between live the aforementioned tartines, as well as grilled cheeses and panini, the preparations that rely on heat—the oven, skillet, grill, broiler—to produce toasty slices, sturdy bases to flank and cradle.

Of course, bread will always win at mopping up the broth as it does for the saffron-infused mussels (see page 136), but the recipes that follow will also show how amenable day-old bread is to various treatments, how the prime of a loaf's life is far from over at the onset of staling, and how quickly, with good bread on hand, a nourishing meal can materialize, whether a spring lunch of herbed ricotta tartines (see page 108), a savory French toast brunch for a crowd (see page 140), or a hearty dinner of crispy-skinned chicken and fresh greens sauced with pan drippings (see page 139).

The one trick to having success here? A sharp, serrated knife. Simple as it sounds, a serrated knife is crucial for preserving the integrity of the loaf while slicing it up.

SUMMER TARTINES
WITH BURRATA, AVOCADO, HERBS, AND SEEDS

MAKES 4 TARTINES

Adding burrata to anything feels like cheating—a surefire way to pique anyone's interest no matter the application. Avocado possesses similarly enticing powers. Unite them on slices of toasty bread and you're well on your way to the makings of a viral Instagram post. To gild the lily, drizzle the layers with a bright, herby sauce laced with seeds, a sharp and textured dressing to cut the creaminess. And before tucking in, be sure to snap that pic.

4 slices peasant bread (see page 22), Quinoa and Flax Bread (page 31), Three Seed Bread (page 28), or Soft Sandwich Bread (page 74), ½ inch thick

1 cup packed finely chopped mixed herbs, such as basil, cilantro, fresh parsley, and tarragon

¼ cup extra-virgin olive oil

2 tablespoons fresh lemon juice

1 tablespoon white balsamic vinegar

¼ teaspoon sea salt

¼ teaspoon sugar

4 teaspoons mixed seeds, such as sesame, poppy, flax, and millet

One 4-ounce ball of burrata, quartered

2 avocados, sliced

1. Preheat the oven to 450°F. Lay the slices of bread directly on oven racks and toast for 5 to 7 minutes, until lightly crisp. Remove from the oven and set aside.

2. In a small bowl, combine the herbs with the oil. Add the fresh lemon juice, vinegar, salt, and sugar. Stir in the seeds. Set aside.

3. Spread a quarter of the burrata over each slice of bread. Spoon a tablespoon of the herb-seed sauce over the top. Fan a quarter of the avocado slices over the burrata and drizzle with more sauce to taste. Serve the tartines with any extra sauce on the side for dipping.

TRUFFLED PÂTÉ
WITH MELBA TOASTS AND QUINCE JAM

MAKES 2¼ CUPS PÂTÉ; SERVES 8 TO 10

Meet your new favorite pantry staple. They are shatteringly crisp and a vehicle for any topping, and once you get used to having these crunchy melba toasts around, you'll never want for store-bought crackers again. Melba toast can be made with any bread and tastes especially good when made with nut and seed breads—the golden hue and textures of the Pumpkin Harvest Bread (page 88) are particularly beautiful and pair well with all sorts of cheese. Be sure to use a sharp serrated knife and day-old or several-days-old bread, as slicing bread thinly is nearly impossible when it's freshly baked. Once cool, these toasts will keep for weeks stored at room temperature in an airtight container.

Classically, melba toasts are served with pâté, and with both on hand, along with a jar of quince jam and a bottle of Champagne, you're well prepared for any impromptu gathering you may find yourself hosting. The chef I worked for at Fork, a restaurant in Philadelphia, made a most memorable truffled duck pâté, a recipe that called not only for many pounds of chicken livers roasted with garlic, shallots, and thyme but also for the meat pulled from two dozen legs of duck confit. Below is a simpler recipe that omits the duck confit but tastes no less rich.

8 tablespoons (1 stick) unsalted butter

4 medium shallots, halved

2 garlic cloves, halved

A few sprigs of fresh thyme

1 pound chicken livers, trimmed of connective tissue

1½ teaspoons kosher salt, plus more as needed

Freshly cracked black pepper to taste

2 tablespoons Grand Marnier

½ cup heavy cream

1 teaspoon truffle oil, plus more as needed

Melted unsalted butter, for covering the pâté

Homemade Melba Toasts (recipe follows)

Quince or other jam, grainy mustard, and cornichons, for serving

1. Preheat the oven to 425°F. Place the butter, shallots, garlic, thyme, and chicken livers on a sheet pan. Season with 1 teaspoon salt and pepper to taste. Roast for about 15 minutes, or until the livers are just cooked through.

2. Remove the pan from the oven and discard the thyme sprigs. Transfer the remaining contents to a food processor. Pour 1 tablespoon Grand Marnier over the sheet pan to deglaze it. Scrape up any browned bits and add them to the food processor.

3. Purée the mixture until completely smooth. Add the cream, the remaining 1 tablespoon of Grand Marnier, and the remaining ½ teaspoon of salt, and purée. Add 1 teaspoon truffle oil and purée again until smooth. Taste and adjust the seasoning with more truffle oil, salt, and pepper as needed. The mixture will be liquidy but will firm up as it chills.

4. Transfer the purée to glass storage jars and cover with a thin layer of melted butter. Serve the paté with melba toasts, quince jam, grainy mustard, and cornichons.

Homemade Melba Toasts

MAKES 2 TO 3 DOZEN

1 loaf of day- or days-old bread, crusts removed

1. Preheat the oven to 250°F. Slice the bread as thinly as possible; the bread should be no thicker than ¼ inch. Cut the slices roughly into 3 × 1-inch pieces, although irregular shapes are fine, too.

2. Lay the pieces on a sheet pan, spreading them out in a single layer. Cook for 30 minutes. Flip and cook for 30 minutes more.

3. Gently squeeze one of the toasts—if it yields, it isn't done. Return the pan to the oven for 15 minutes, then test again. Remove the pan from the oven and transfer the melba toasts to a cooling rack. Once the toasts are completely cool, after about 1 hour, store them for weeks in airtight containers.

ENDIVE AND FAVA SALAD TARTINES
WITH HERBED RICOTTA

MAKES 6 TARTINES

One March day several years ago, my aunt and I stopped into Burlington, Vermont's South End Kitchen, an adorable café serving simple, local fare. Bundled in our warmest gear for the outing, braving the snowy roads hugging a frozen-solid Lake Champlain, we relished the tartine we ordered that afternoon—ricotta, pea shoots, radishes, and herbs—each spring-filled bite assuring us we could endure a few more weeks of winter. This is the tartine to make when you've had your fill of comfort foods—of soups and stews and roasts and braises—and you long for something fresh and bright. Favas are a laborious treat but can be hard to find; frozen edamame work just as well.

2 tablespoons minced shallots

Kosher salt

Pinch of sugar

2 tablespoons white balsamic vinegar

1 pound fava beans, or a heaping ½ cup shelled edamame

2 heads endive (3 ounces each), julienned

2 scallions, white and green parts thinly sliced to yield about 2 tablespoons

6 radishes, thinly sliced

⅓ cup extra-virgin olive oil, plus more for drizzling

½ cup fresh basil leaves

1 cup fresh ricotta

½ cup finely chopped mixed fresh herbs, such as dill, chives, and fresh parsley

Zest of 1 lemon

Freshly cracked black pepper to taste

6 slices bread, such as peasant bread (see page 22), Quinoa and Flax Bread (page 31), Three Seed Bread (page 28), or Soft Sandwich Bread (page 74), ¾ inch thick

1. In a small bowl, season the shallots with a pinch each of salt and sugar. Cover with vinegar and let sit for 10 minutes.

2. Meanwhile, bring a large pot of water to a boil over high heat. Shell the fava beans, then drop them in the water and cook for 1 minute. Drain and plunge them into an ice bath. Peel the favas and set aside. If you're using edamame, boil for 1 minute, then plunge into the ice bath.

3. In a large bowl combine the endive, scallions, radishes, and favas. Whisk ⅓ cup oil into the vinegar mixture, pour it over the vegetables, and toss to coat. Taste and adjust the seasoning with salt, as needed. If you have small, tender basil leaves, add them to the bowl whole; otherwise, roughly chop the leaves, add them to the bowl, and toss to coat.

4. In a small bowl, stir together the ricotta, mixed herbs, and lemon zest. Season with salt and pepper to taste.

5. Preheat the broiler to high. Arrange the bread on a sheet pan and drizzle with oil. Turn the slices over and drizzle with more oil. Transfer to the oven and broil for about 2 minutes, until golden, keeping an eye on them to prevent burning. Flip and broil the other side until golden, 1 to 2 minutes more. Transfer the bread to a serving board or platter.

6. Spread each slice of bread with ricotta and mound the endive salad on top. Serve immediately.

CABBAGE SOUP
WITH GRUYÈRE-RYE TOASTS

SERVES 6

Why should French onion soup have all the fun? Few soups *don't* thrive under a blanket of bubbling cheese-crusted toast. Here, thick slices of rye bread dry out in the oven as the soup simmers stovetop. The toasts finish under the broiler with Gruyère and a grating of nutmeg. If you don't have a set of oven-safe soup bowls, simply run the cheese toasts under the broiler on a sheet pan, then float them atop piping-hot soup before serving.

6 slices Rye Bread (page 48), or your choice of bread, 1 inch thick

6 cups thinly sliced green cabbage

2 ounces diced pancetta

⅓ cup extra-virgin olive oil

6 cups sliced sweet onions (about 1½ pounds)

Kosher salt to taste

2 teaspoons whole caraway seeds

1 teaspoon sugar

¼ cup white balsamic or white wine vinegar

6 cups homemade Chicken Stock (page 183)

Freshly cracked black pepper

2 cups grated Gruyère, Emmental, or Comté cheese

Freshly grated nutmeg (optional)

1. Preheat the oven to 200°F. Lay the bread slices directly on the oven racks and let them dry out while you make the soup. The bread can stay in the oven like this for as long as an hour.

2. Bring a large pot of water to a boil over high heat. Add the cabbage and cook for 1 minute, then drain but don't clean the large pot.

3. Meanwhile, in a large sauté pan, cook the pancetta over medium heat until it is crisp and the fat is rendered. Add the oil and onions and season with a pinch of salt. Sauté, stirring occasionally, about 10 minutes, or until golden.

4. In the large pot used to cook the cabbage, combine the drained cabbage, caraway seeds, sugar, vinegar, stock, a pinch of salt, and pepper to taste over medium heat. Add the sautéed onions and pancetta. Bring the soup to a boil, then reduce the heat to low and simmer for 10 minutes, or until it tastes sweet with a subtle bite. Taste and adjust the seasoning as needed.

5. Remove the bread from the oven and preheat the broiler to high. Ladle the soup into individual oven-safe bowls and place the slices of bread on top. Cover the bread with the grated cheese, dividing it evenly. Sprinkle with the nutmeg, if using.

6. Arrange the bowls on a sheet pan and place the pan under the broiler. Broil for 5 minutes, watching closely to prevent it from burning, or until the cheese is bubbling and lightly golden. Remove the pan from the broiler and serve the soup immediately.

SEAFOOD BISQUE
IN BREAD BOWLS

SERVES 4

For the same reason it makes good sense to buy whole chickens, it's wise to buy shell-on shrimp: free stock! When covered with water and simmered with a few seasonings, shrimp shells produce an intense-flavored stock in a mere 45 minutes. As the stock reduces on the stovetop, soup preparations can begin: peel, dice, chop, sauté. In no time, a light, creamy bisque, filled with vegetables, shrimp, and flaky white fish, will materialize. Of course, you do not have to make the bread bowls (see page 77), though I highly recommend you do—isn't every soup infinitely more exciting when served in a crusty bowl of bread?

for the shrimp stock

1 pound shell-on wild shrimp

1 bay leaf

3 celery stalks, roughly chopped

1 onion, roughly chopped

2 carrots, scrubbed and roughly chopped

Pinch of kosher salt

for the bisque

2 tablespoons extra-virgin olive oil

2 cups finely diced onions (about 2 medium onions)

1 cup finely diced celery

Kosher salt

1 cup dry white wine

1 pound red potatoes, peeled and cut into ¼-inch dice

1 pound white fish fillets, such as hake, cod, or haddock, skin removed, cut into 1-inch pieces

1 cup heavy cream

2 tablespoons finely chopped fresh dill, or more to taste

Freshly cracked black pepper to taste

4 Soup Bread Bowls (page 77) (optional), for serving

1. Make the shrimp stock: Peel the shrimp and place the shells in a large stockpot over high heat; reserve the shrimp for the bisque. Add 6 cups water, the bay leaf, celery, onion, carrots, and a pinch of salt. Bring to a boil, then reduce the heat to low and gently simmer for 45 minutes. Strain the stock, discarding the shells, bay leaf, and vegetables. You should have about 3 cups. If you don't, add enough water to make 3 cups.

2. Make the bisque: Heat the oil in a large pot over high heat. When it begins to shimmer, add the onion, celery, and a pinch of salt. Stir to distribute, cover the pot, and immediately reduce the heat to low. Cook for 15 minutes without touching the pot until the vegetables are soft.

3. Remove the lid, increase the heat to medium, add the wine, and simmer for 5 minutes, just until the wine has reduced slightly. Add the potatoes, shrimp stock, 1 teaspoon salt, and 3 cups water. Increase the heat to medium high and bring to a boil, then reduce the heat to low so that the liquid is gently simmering. Simmer for about 20 minutes, or until the potatoes are cooked.

4. Cut the shrimp into ½-inch pieces. Add them to the pot along with the fish. Add the cream, dill, and pepper to taste. Bring the bisque to a simmer. Taste and add more salt, if necessary. Ladle the bisque into the bread bowls and serve them immediately.

NOTE: Shrimp stock can be made ahead and refrigerated for 3 days or frozen for 3 months. If you don't want to make the shrimp stock, substitute chicken stock.

EGGPLANT CAPONATA
WITH TAHINI SAUCE AND GRILLED BREAD

SERVES 8 TO 10 AS AN APPETIZER

This is what happens when Yotam Ottolenghi takes over your bookshelves: your caponata migrates east, welcoming cumin, za'atar, and mint to the riot of eggplant, tomato, and onion; a drizzle of tahini sauce makes everything better. You can serve the caponata immediately, but if you have time, make it ahead—its flavors meld and develop as it sits for a day or two. Incidentally, this whole ensemble happens to be vegan, but with its textures, colors, and flavors, no one will miss the meat (though a block of feta wouldn't hurt).

¼ cup extra-virgin olive oil, plus more for drizzling

8 cups ¾-inch-diced eggplant (about 2 medium)

1 heaping cup diced onion

Kosher salt and freshly cracked black pepper to taste

2 cups diced tomatoes (1 to 2 tomatoes)

2 garlic cloves, minced

½ teaspoon ground cumin

1½ teaspoons za'atar, plus more for serving

2 tablespoons vinegar (white balsamic, white wine, or red wine)

2 tablespoons capers

⅓ cup toasted pine nuts (see Note)

½ cup finely chopped fresh parsley

2 tablespoons finely chopped fresh mint

⅓ cup golden raisins

1 tablespoon fresh lemon juice

1 loaf of bread, such as peasant bread (see page 22), Three Seed Bread (page 28), or Walnut Bread (page 36), sliced ½ inch thick

Tahini Sauce (recipe follows)

1. In a large, wide sauté pan, heat ¼ cup oil over high heat. When it begins to shimmer, add the eggplant and onion—the pot will feel very full. Season with a generous pinch of salt and pepper to taste. Cover, immediately reduce the heat to low, and cook for 20 minutes—no need to lift the lid and stir during this time.

2. Add the tomatoes, garlic, cumin, and za'atar to the pan with the eggplant and onion, raise the heat to medium, and simmer for 7 to 10 minutes, until the liquid begins to evaporate and the vegetables begin to stick to the pan. Add the vinegar and capers and stir, scraping the bottom of the pan for about 1 minute. Remove the pan from the heat. Add the toasted pine nuts, parsley, mint, golden raisins, and lemon juice. Taste and adjust the seasoning with more salt and pepper as needed. Set aside to cool.

3. Preheat a grill or grill pan to high. Drizzle both sides of bread slices with olive oil, and grill until lightly charred and crisp, 1 to 2 minutes a side. Arrange on a platter. Spoon the caponata on top of the bread, drizzle with tahini sauce, and sprinkle with za'atar. Serve the caponata immediately.

NOTE: In a small dry skillet, toast pine nuts over low heat, tossing frequently, until golden, about 5 minutes. Immediately transfer them to a bowl and set aside.

Tahini Sauce

MAKES ⅔ CUP

3 tablespoons well-stirred tahini paste

3 tablespoons extra-virgin olive oil

2 teaspoons fresh lemon juice
  (from about ½ a lemon)

¼ teaspoon kosher salt, plus more to taste

1 to 2 garlic cloves, minced

1 teaspoon maple syrup, honey, or sugar

In a small bowl, combine the tahini paste with
the oil, lemon juice, ¼ teaspoon salt, garlic, and
2 tablespoons water. Add the maple syrup. Taste and
adjust with more salt as needed and thin out with
more water, too, if necessary—the sauce should be
pourable or the consistency of a traditional dressing.

BRUSCHETTA
WITH TOMATOES, CARAWAY, AND BASIL

MAKES 6 BRUSCHETTA

The dish I associate most with introducing me to the joys of bread-as-utensil is my grandfather's tomato feast: slices dressed in oil and vinegar, seasoned with dried basil, thyme, and caraway. I never thought twice about the use of dried herbs at the time—I didn't know any differently—and my mother never strayed from her father's recipe because my siblings and I all loved it. By the end of every evening, when just a few slices of tomatoes lingered on the oval platter set in the center of the porch table, hands from all directions reached in, tipping the platter to pool the juices as needed, bread always leading the way. Today I use the same flavors as in my grandfather's salad to make bruschetta, seasoning the tomatoes lightly with fresh thyme and caraway, a subtle but welcomed earthiness to complement the sweet fresh basil and tomatoes.

1½ pounds tomatoes (about 3 large), diced into
    ½-inch cubes

Sea salt and freshly cracked black pepper

½ teaspoon caraway seeds

½ teaspoon minced fresh thyme

1 tablespoon minced fresh basil

2 tablespoons extra-virgin olive oil, plus more for
    drizzling

1 tablespoon white balsamic vinegar

6 slices peasant bread (see page 22), Three Seed
    Bread (page 28), or Roasted Garlic Bread (page 49),
    ½ inch thick

1 garlic clove, halved

1. Preheat the oven to 450°F. In a large bowl, season the tomatoes with ½ teaspoon salt and ¼ teaspoon pepper. Scatter the caraway, thyme, and basil on top. Drizzle with 2 tablespoons oil and the vinegar and let stand for 10 minutes.

2. Arrange the bread on a rimmed sheet pan and drizzle lightly on both sides with oil. Transfer the pan to the oven and toast for 7 to 10 minutes, until evenly golden. Remove the bread from the oven and rub it with the halved garlic. Set the bread on a large cutting board or serving platter.

3. Gently toss the tomato mixture. Taste and add more salt, pepper, and herbs, if necessary. Spoon the tomato mixture evenly over the toasts. Cut the toasts in half and serve.

ALMOND- AND PLUM-BUTTER SANDWICHES

MAKES 4 SANDWICHES

Making any kind of nut butter is an exercise in faith and patience. Just when your food processor feels hot to the touch and the smell of a burning engine overtakes the scent of toasty nuts, the paste jammed into the corner yields and the swirling mass lets down, instantly becoming liquidy. This process typically takes six minutes, at which point you can flavor the nut butter as you please. The beauty is the control you have over everything: the quality of the nuts, the type of flavorings, the degree to which you want to push that irresistibly salty-sweet dynamic.

This almond butter, sweetened with maple syrup, pairs particularly well with homemade plum butter, a vanilla-scented spread my mother has made in large batches every summer for as long as I can remember. It is not at all similar to the spiced, dark spreads the words *fruit butter* evoke, but more like a less-sweet jam, fresh and fragrant, with the most brilliant ruby hue. The recipe takes some time to make but produces a huge quantity, plenty to have on hand for weeks plus enough to share with friends—it makes a wonderful gift and a superlative PB&J.

for the plum butter

2 pounds firm, but not quite ripe, black-skinned plums, quartered, stones removed

2 tablespoons lemon juice

½ vanilla bean, split lengthwise

1½ cups sugar

for the almond butter

2 cups almonds

1 tablespoon melted coconut oil, plus more as needed

1 tablespoon maple syrup

½ teaspoons kosher salt, plus more as needed

for assembly

8 slices Soft Sandwich Bread (page 74), ½ inch thick

(recipe continues)

1. Make the plum butter: Preheat the oven to 375°F. Place three or four small plates and silver or metal spoons in the freezer. In a 4-quart pot, combine the plums, 2 tablespoons water, and the lemon juice. Scrape in the seeds of the split vanilla bean and toss in the pod, too. Bring it to a boil slowly over medium heat, keeping an eye on it to prevent scorching. Reduce the heat to low, cover, and cook, checking and stirring frequently, until the fruit is very soft, about 20 minutes. Remove and discard the vanilla pod.

2. Meanwhile, make the almond butter: Lay the almonds on a sheet pan, spreading them in a single layer, and roast them in the oven for 10 to 12 minutes, until lightly browned and fragrant. Remove the pan from the oven and let the almonds cool briefly, about 5 minutes.

3. Transfer the nuts to a food processor and purée until liquidy, about 6 minutes. Scrape down the sides with a spatula and continue puréeing. With the machine running, drizzle in the coconut oil. Drizzle in the maple syrup, which will make the mixture thicken. Add the salt and continue puréeing. Taste and add more salt if necessary. Add more coconut oil by the teaspoon if the texture needs thinning. Transfer the almond butter to a glass storage vessel.

4. Set a food mill over a large bowl, and purée the plums, along with their juice, in batches. Return the strained purée to a clean large pot. Place it over medium heat, add the sugar, and stir until dissolved. Increase the heat to high, bring the fruit to a boil, then reduce the heat to a very low simmer. Stirring frequently, simmer uncovered for about 1 hour.

5. To test for doneness, dip a cold spoon from the freezer into the boiling mixture and pour a spoonful onto one of the cold plates. Return the plate to the freezer for a few minutes, then run your finger through the jam. If the little trench stays intact without the jam creeping back together, the plum butter is done. Otherwise, continue to cook, checking every 10 minutes until it passes this test.

6. Pour the plum butter into glass jars and allow it to cool completely at room temperature, 2 to 3 hours. Cover the jars and refrigerate until ready to use.

7. Assemble the sandwiches: Lay 8 slices of bread on a large clean surface. Spread about 1 tablespoon of almond butter evenly over each of 4 slices of bread. Spread about 1 tablespoon of plum butter on each of the remaining 4 slices of bread. Sandwich the slices together and serve.

NOTE: Both the plum butter and almond butter can be made ahead and stored—the plum butter in the fridge for up to 2 weeks, the almond butter at room temperature for the same amount of time. The plum butter recipe also doubles well. When scaling, measure the purée after it has been strained, and for each cup of purée, use ½ cup sugar.

TARRAGON CHICKEN SALAD SANDWICHES

MAKES 4 SANDWICHES

Thien Ngo, the chef I worked for at Fork, a restaurant in Philadelphia, used the same technique for boiling chickens as potatoes: submerge in a pot of cold water, bring to a boil, turn off the heat, and let cool completely in the liquid. This method ensures the chicken (or potatoes) will not be overcooked, and better yet, will be *perfectly* cooked. What's more, when the meat is removed and the chicken carcass is further simmered in the poaching liquid, it yields an abundant stock for future use (see Note). Here, a homemade tarragon mayonnaise, which takes no time to make in the food processor, dresses the pulled meat, and quick-pickled onions add bite, texture, and a beautiful rosy hue to these sandwiches. If you make the onions a day in advance, the flavor and color will intensify in the best possible way.

for the tarragon chicken

One 3- to 4-pound chicken

Kosher salt

Freshly cracked black pepper to taste

Tarragon Mayonnaise (recipe follows)

Lemon juice (optional)

for the quick pickled onion

1 small red onion, thinly sliced

Kosher salt

1 tablespoon white balsamic vinegar

for assembly

8 slices bread, such as Three Seed Bread (page 28), Soft Sandwich Bread (page 74), or Quinoa and Flax Bread (page 31), ½ inch thick

Arugula or other greens

NOTE: To make chicken stock, return the skin and bones to the pot of poaching liquid. Add 1 teaspoon kosher salt, bring to a boil, then reduce the heat and simmer, uncovered, for 2 to 3 hours, until the stock tastes flavorful. Let it cool with the bones in the pot. Remove and discard the bones and strain the stock into a clean pot or bowl. Refrigerate overnight, then skim off the fat. Store the stock in freezer containers for up to 3 months.

(recipe continues)

1. Make the tarragon chicken: Place the chicken in a large pot. Cover it with cold water, being sure the chicken is completely submerged. Bring it to a boil, uncovered, over high heat, then turn off the heat. Cover the pot and let it sit for 1 hour. Remove the chicken from the pot and pull the meat from the bones; some chicken will cling to the bones. (To make stock, do not discard the bones, fat, or poaching water; see Note on page 121.)

2. Cut the pulled meat into bite-size pieces, then place it in a large bowl. Season with ½ teaspoon kosher salt and pepper to taste. Toss with tarragon mayonnaise to taste. Taste and adjust the seasoning with more salt and pepper as needed. Add lemon juice to taste, if using. Chill until ready to assemble the sandwiches.

3. Make the quick pickled onion: Place the onion in a small bowl. Season the onion with a pinch of salt, and cover it with the vinegar. Let it sit for at least 10 minutes at room temperature or up to a day in the refrigerator.

4. Assemble the sandwiches: Top 4 slices of bread with chicken salad, pickled onion, and greens. Top them with the remaining slices of bread. Serve the sandwiches immediately.

Tarragon Mayonnaise

MAKES 1¼ CUPS

If using a raw egg worries you, you can boil the egg for 4 minutes before cracking it into the food processor.

1 egg

2 teaspoons Dijon mustard

1 tablespoon vinegar, preferably white balsamic vinegar

¼ cup fresh tarragon leaves

½ teaspoon kosher salt

Freshly cracked black pepper to taste

1 cup neutral oil

In the bowl of a food processor, combine the egg, mustard, vinegar, tarragon, salt, and pepper, and purée until smooth. With the motor running, add the oil in a slow, steady stream. Scrape down the sides of the bowl. The mixture will be thick and pale green. Taste and adjust the seasoning as needed.

CRAB SALAD SANDWICHES
WITH SAUCE GRIBICHE

MAKES 4 SANDWICHES

The late Judy Rodgers passed along so many gems in *The Zuni Café Cookbook*, but none greater than 4-minute egg *gribiche*, which she describes as an herby, shalloty mayonnaise—a sauce she suggests serving with anything from sandwiches to grilled fish, poultry to fried shrimp, and boiled potatoes to cracked crab. A barely cooked egg binds this undulant, creamy sauce, which, with minor tweaks, quickly transmutes into other favorite sauces: with minced anchovies and lemon or vinegar, it becomes a Caesar dressing; with masses of garlic, an aioli; with capers and cornichons, a tartar sauce. But it's nearly perfect on its own, too, and just as Rodgers promised, it makes a memorable crab salad.

1 large egg

2 tablespoons finely diced shallots

2 tablespoons white balsamic vinegar

¼ teaspoon kosher salt, plus more as needed

2 teaspoons Dijon mustard

1 cup neutral oil

¼ cup finely chopped chives

1 tablespoon capers, roughly chopped

1 pound jumbo lump crabmeat, picked over

Spring greens or Boston lettuce

8 slices bread, such as Three Seed Bread (page 28), Soft Sandwich Bread (page 74), or Quinoa and Flax Bread (page 31), ½ inch thick

1. Bring a small pot of water to a simmer over high heat. Lower the egg into the water, return the water to a boil, then reduce the heat to medium and simmer for 4 minutes. Transfer the egg to a small bowl of cold water.

2. Meanwhile, in a small bowl, place the shallots and cover them with the vinegar. Let them macerate for 10 minutes.

3. When the egg is cool, crack it and scrape it into the bowl of a food processor. Add the salt and mustard. With the motor running, stream in the oil; the mixture should be as thick as mayonnaise. Transfer the mixture to a medium bowl and stir in the chives, capers, and the shallot and vinegar mixture. Taste and add more salt, if necessary. Set aside.

4. In a large bowl, place the crabmeat. Add ½ cup dressing and, with your hands, gently toss the crabmeat, taking care not to break up the lumps and turn the mixture to mush. Taste and adjust with more dressing and salt as needed. Leftover dressing can be refrigerated, covered, for up to 3 days.

5. To prepare the sandwiches, lay lettuce on 4 slices of bread, top each with a mound of crab salad, and close the sandwiches with the remaining bread slices.

SOPPRESSATA, PROVOLONE, AND PEPERONATA SANDWICHES

MAKES 12 SANDWICHES; MAKES 3 CUPS PEPERONATA

Halved crosswise, spread with layers of cheese and cured meat, and topped with a sweet-tart *peperonata,* a mixture of peppers and onions, homemade focaccia can feed a crowd. With its crisp, oily crust, focaccia holds up well under the layers of cheese, meat, and sauce, allowing these sandwiches to be made ahead of time. Wrap them tightly in wax paper and pack them to go, or secure them with sandwich picks and present them on your largest board: this is tailgating, potlucking, and picnicking fare at its finest.

for the peperonata

¼ cup extra-virgin olive oil

3 bell peppers, seeded and sliced ¼ inch thick (about 6 cups)

2 cups sliced onion (about 1 large onion)

2 garlic cloves, minced

Pinch of kosher salt

2 tablespoons white balsamic, white wine, or cider vinegar

2 tablespoons capers

¼ cup thinly sliced fresh basil

for assembly

1 recipe plain focaccia (see page 68) or a 1-pound sheet, cut into 12 squares

9 ounces soppressata or salami

Grainy mustard, for serving (optional)

12 ounces sliced Provolone

1. Make the *peperonata:* In a large skillet, heat the oil over high heat. When it begins to shimmer, add the peppers and onions, and immediately reduce the heat to low. Add the garlic and season with a pinch of salt. Cover the pan and cook for 20 minutes, stirring once halfway through. You should hear a slight sizzle the entire time.

2. Remove the lid, give everything a stir, increase the heat to medium, and cook, uncovered, for 2 minutes more. Add the vinegar and capers, stir, and cook for 1 minute more, or until the juices have reduced. Add the fresh basil, stir, and remove the pan from the heat. Set it aside to cool.

3. Assemble the sandwiches: Halve each piece of focaccia crosswise. Lay slices of soppressata over each bottom half of focaccia. Spread mustard over each top, if using. Top the soppressata with *peperonata,* then layer the Provolone on top. Close the sandwiches, securing with sandwich picks, if necessary.

NOTE: Try assembling these sandwiches as one large slab: Trim the ends off each of the focaccia's four sides. Use a serrated knife to halve the sheet crosswise to create two large rectangles. Shingle slices of soppressata over the entire bottom surface, then top with the *peperonata* and layer the slices of Provolone. Spread mustard, if using, on the underside of the top focaccia layer, then close the sandwich. Present the assembled slab on a large board and cut into individual sandwiches just before serving.

BACON, CHEDDAR, AND ONION JAM PANINI

MAKES 4 SANDWICHES

In *Laws of Cooking: And How to Break Them*, chef Justin Warner distills the widely adored PB&J into three basic elements: something sweet (jelly), something rich (peanut butter), and something to spread it on (bread). This union of fat and fruit on a canvas is the foundation of his first law of cooking, the law of peanut butter and jelly, which he uses to explain our universal love for so many foods. This addictive panini, a meeting of sweet-sharp onion jam and rich bacon and cheese flanked by toasty bread, can similarly be explained. The key to making the onion jam is to be patient while cooking the onions: they should be meltingly tender and beginning to caramelize before adding the sugar, wine, and vinegar, which will ensure the finished product is absent of any raw onion taste. Be sure to plan ahead—the onion jam cooks for nearly 2 hours. Other sweet-tart fruity jams such as lingonberry or rhubarb can be used in its place.

8 ounces bacon

8 slices Soft Sandwich Bread (page 74), ½ inch thick

4 heaping tablespoons Onion Jam (recipe follows)

Mayonnaise to taste (optional)

4 slices Cheddar cheese

Reserved bacon grease, neutral oil, or a mixture of mayonnaise and softened salted butter (see page 128), for cooking the sandwiches

---

NOTE: A spoonful of onion jam will brighten any wintry panini such as the bacon and Cheddar one featured here, but it's also a nice complement to summer tartines: spread the onion jam over grilled or broiled bread and top it with slices of balsamic-roasted eggplant or fresh tomatoes and sea salt or slivers of roasted red peppers and crumbled goat cheese.

1. Preheat the oven to 425°F. Lay the bacon on a sheet pan, separating and spacing each slice. Transfer to the oven and cook for 12 to 15 minutes, until lightly crisped. Remove the pan from the oven and transfer the bacon to a paper-towel-lined plate to drain. Reserve the rendered bacon fat for cooking, if desired.

2. Heat a panini machine, griddle, or large skillet over medium heat. Lay the slices of bread on a clean surface. Spread 1 heaping tablespoon of the onion jam over each of 4 slices of bread. Spread mayonnaise, if using, on the remaining 4 slices of bread. Top the onion jam with 2 or 3 slices of bacon and 1 slice of Cheddar cheese. Close the sandwiches with the other 4 slices of bread.

3. Brush the outsides of the bread with about 2 teaspoons of rendered bacon fat, neutral oil, or a mayonnaise-butter mixture. Place the sandwiches in the panini machine or on top of the griddle or skillet. If you are not using a panini machine, weigh down the sandwiches with another heavy pan or object. Cook the sandwiches until golden, about 2 minutes, checking after 1 minute to ensure they are browning evenly. Flip them and cook for another 2 minutes, or until golden—but don't weigh down the sandwiches on the second side. If you are using a panini press, there is no need to flip the sandwiches—simply cook them until the bread is golden and the cheese is melting. Remove the sandwiches and let them rest briefly before cutting and serving them.

Onion Jam

MAKES 1 CUP

2 tablespoons extra-virgin olive oil

5 to 6 cups finely diced onions (about 1½ pounds)

Kosher salt

1 tablespoon sugar

1 cup white wine

¼ cup white wine vinegar or white balsamic vinegar

1. In a large skillet, heat the oil over high heat. When it begins to shimmer, add the onions and a pinch of salt, cover the pan, reduce the heat to low, and cook for 20 minutes. Uncover, give the onions a stir, and continue cooking over low heat for 1 hour, or until they just begin to caramelize. Increase the heat to medium, add the sugar, and cook for 2 minutes more, or until the sugar dissolves.

2. Increase the heat to high, add the wine, bring to a simmer, then reduce the heat to low, and cook until the wine has nearly evaporated, 20 to 25 minutes. Add the vinegar, and cook until the liquid has been reduced to a syrupy consistency and the onions have a jam-like consistency, about 10 minutes more. The mixture should taste at once sharp and sweet. Add more salt to taste. Store, covered, in the refrigerator for up to 1 week.

FOOD CART GRILLED CHEESE

MAKES 4 SANDWICHES

Several summers ago, my family spent a long weekend in South Portland, Maine, just a short drive away from Bite into Maine, a food cart perched on a hill in Fort Williams Park. Lobster rolls, of course, drew us to the idyllic spot, set on a sweeping lawn disappearing into the Atlantic, an iconic lighthouse towering over the whole breezy scene—blankets, dogs, Frisbees, kites. We visited daily, savoring every bite of the squishy rolls teeming with fresh, sweet claw meat, but by the end of the weekend, we found ourselves just as taken by their no-frills grilled cheese, the perfectly toasted white bread, the just-melted Cheddar cheese, the absence of any fancy sauce. Making a really good grilled cheese is no small feat, but with good technique and ingredients, it can be easily achieved at home:

- Use salted butter—Bite into Maine owners Sarah and Karl Sutton use Cabot—for an exceptionally tasty exterior.

- Mix the salted butter with a little mayonnaise, which has a higher smoke point than butter and will allow the bread to crisp evenly without burning.

- Lacquer the bread, edge to edge, not the cooking surface.

- Use a good, flavorful melting cheese such as Cheddar, Gruyère, Comté, Emmental, fontina, or Monterey Jack. When I make these for my children, I use a mild Cheddar, as they do at Bite into Maine. Sliced cheese as opposed to grated, moreover, makes assembly easy.

- Use something heavy such as a large skillet to weigh down the sandwich as it cooks, helping the cheese melt about as quickly as the bread toasts.

4 tablespoons (½ stick) salted butter, softened

2 tablespoons mayonnaise

8 slices Soft Sandwich Bread (page 74), peasant bread (see page 22), or Cheesy Cheddar and Parmigiano Bread (page 52), ½ inch thick

8 slices mild Cheddar cheese

1. Heat a griddle or large cast-iron or steel skillet over medium heat.

2. In a medium bowl, beat the butter and mayonnaise together with a spoon or spatula until well blended. Spread about 2 teaspoons of the mixture evenly over one side of each slice of bread, crust to crust. Layer 2 slices of cheese on the non-buttered side of 4 slices, and close the sandwiches with the remaining slices so that buttered sides of bread are facing out.

3. Lay the sandwiches on the hot griddle or skillet. Weigh down the sandwiches with another heavy object and cook until golden, about 2 minutes, checking after 1 minute to ensure they are browning evenly. Flip and cook the sandwiches for another 2 minutes, or until they are golden—don't weigh down the sandwiches on the second side. Remove the sandwiches from the heat, and let them rest for 2 minutes before cutting in half and serving them.

VINAIGRETTE TOASTS
WITH SOFT-BOILED EGGS

MAKES 4 TOASTS

Treating your toast to an oil-and-vinegar bath in place of an egg-and-milk custard may at first glance strike you as unfamiliar. But if you think about why you love dragging your bread across the dregs of your salad plate or why you love a panzanella salad, the idea doesn't feel so foreign. Here, slices of vinaigrette-soaked bread sear first on the stovetop, then finish in the oven, where the bite of the vinegar tempers as the toasts crisp. The creamy yolk of a six-minute egg rounds it all out, a union of sweet, sharp, and smooth.

4 tablespoons extra-virgin olive oil

2 tablespoons vinegar, preferably white balsamic

4 slices Soft Sandwich Bread (page 74), ¾ inch thick

4 eggs

Sea salt and freshly cracked black pepper to taste

1. Preheat the oven to 425°F. Bring a small saucepan filled with water to a boil over high heat. In a 9 × 13-inch baking pan, whisk together 3 tablespoons oil with the vinegar. Lay the slices of bread in the pan, let them sit for 1 minute, then flip and let them sit for another minute or until the oil and vinegar are completely absorbed.

2. In a large ovenproof sauté pan, heat the remaining tablespoon oil over medium heat. When it begins to shimmer, carefully lower the bread into the pan. Cook until the underside of the bread is golden, about 5 minutes. Flip the slices and immediately transfer the pan to the oven for 5 minutes or until the slices are evenly golden.

3. Meanwhile, carefully lower the eggs into the saucepan with boiling water and reduce the heat to low so that the water is gently simmering. Cook the eggs for 6 minutes, or according to your preference. Remove the eggs from the saucepan with a slotted spoon and transfer them to a bowl of cold water.

4. To serve, set 1 toast on each plate. Crack and scoop out an egg over each piece. Season with salt and pepper to taste.

LEEK, HAM, AND EMMENTAL CROQUE MADAME

MAKES 4 TARTINES

When heavy cream reduces briefly on the stovetop, it thickens and attains a béchamel-like nature. This shortcut allows croque monsieur (the classic French broiled or fried ham-and-cheese sandwich) or madame (the same sandwich topped with an egg) to materialize in a fraction of the time required when a "proper" béchamel is used. Here, leeks sweat in butter and water until soft, then meld with ham, Emmental, and our thickened cream before uniting with the runny yolk of a sunny-side-up egg. Serve it with a salad for dinner—and don't think twice about your smart, if rich, shortcut. Any leftover leek mixture can be saved for tucking in to an omelet or spreading across a pizza.

4 cups thinly sliced leeks, soaked and drained (see Note, page 182)

3 tablespoons unsalted butter

Pinch of kosher salt

Freshly cracked black pepper to taste

4 slices bread, such as peasant bread (see page 22), Cheesy Cheddar and Parmigiano Bread (page 52), or Walnut Bread (page 36), ½ inch thick

2 slices ham, diced to yield about ¼ cup

¼ cup heavy cream

1½ cups grated Emmental or Gruyère cheese

4 eggs

Minced fresh thyme

1. In a large sauté pan over high heat, combine the leeks, 2 tablespoons butter, and 2 tablespoons water. Season with a pinch of salt and pepper to taste. As soon as you hear a sizzle, cover the pan, and reduce the heat to low. Cook for about 15 minutes, or until tender, peeking halfway to ensure the liquid has not evaporated. If the mixture looks dry, add another tablespoon of water.

2. Meanwhile, preheat the broiler to high. Set two cooling racks on a rimmed sheet pan. Place the bread slices on the cooling racks and broil until golden, about 2 minutes. Flip and broil the other side until golden, 1 to 2 minutes more, keeping a close watch so they don't burn. Remove the pan from the oven and set it aside. Keep the broiler on.

3. Uncover the pan with leeks and increase the heat to medium. Cook the leeks, now stirring constantly, for 1 minute more to allow any remaining liquid to cook away. Add the diced ham, cream, and ¼ cup cheese, and cook until the cream bubbles and thickens and the cheese melts, 1 to 2 minutes. Add pepper to taste and stir, then remove the pan from the heat and set aside.

4. In a large skillet melt the remaining 1 tablespoon butter over medium heat, tilting the pan to coat it. Crack in the eggs and cook until the whites are almost set but the yolks are still runny, about 1 minute.

5. Meanwhile, spread about ¼ cup of the leek mixture over each toast, being sure to spread it to the edges. Sprinkle a pinch of thyme over each. Slide 1 egg on top. Divide the remaining cheese equally over the toasts.

6. Return the sheet pan to the oven and broil the toasts again until the cheese is bubbling and slightly golden, about 2 minutes.

MUSSELS
WITH SAFFRON, CRÈME FRAÎCHE, AND GRILLED OLIVE OIL TOASTS

SERVES 2

I don't think there exists a dish better suited to sop up with crusty bread than mussels. In this version, saffron, the dried stigma from a purple crocus, tinges the broth yellow-orange and imparts a floral, somewhat bitter flavor. Because of its labor-intensive production, which requires careful hand-picking, saffron is expensive. Classically it is used in seafood stews throughout southern France, and while it certainly is a worthwhile investment, it can easily be omitted here—the shallot, wine, and butter broth enriched with crème fraîche is quite lovely on its own.

Pinch of saffron (¼ to ½ teaspoon)

½ cup dry white wine

4 tablespoons (½ stick) unsalted butter

½ cup finely minced shallots

2 garlic cloves, thinly sliced

4 tablespoons crème fraîche

Sea salt and freshly cracked black pepper to taste

2 pounds mussels, rinsed and scrubbed

½ cup finely minced fresh parsley

4 slices peasant bread (see page 22),
  ½ inch thick

Extra-virgin olive oil, for drizzling

1. In a small bowl, crumble the saffron over the white wine. Set aside.

2. In a large pot, melt the butter over medium heat. Stir in the shallots and garlic. When they begin sizzling, cover the pot, reduce the heat to low, and cook for 15 minutes.

3. Preheat a grill or grill pan on high.

4. Uncover the pot and increase the heat to high. Add the saffron-infused wine and crème fraîche and stir to combine. Season with a pinch of salt and pepper to taste. When the liquid comes to a simmer, add the mussels, cover the pot, and cook for 3 to 5 minutes, until the mussels open; discard any that do not. Add the parsley and stir to incorporate.

5. Drizzle the bread with oil. Lay the slices on the grill or grill pan and toast until lightly charred, about 2 minutes. Flip and toast the bread 1 to 2 minutes more. Serve the mussels immediately with grilled toasts alongside to sop up the broth.

ROAST CHICKEN LEGS AND TOAST

SERVES 4

Judy Rodgers's roast chicken and bread salad from *The Zuni Café Cookbook* is the ultimate kitchen endeavor. Beginning with salting the chicken three days in advance, to roasting it for an hour, to dressing a bread salad with the utmost attention, the result is to be savored slowly, each bite of crispy-skinned chicken, every morsel of chewy bread. In this pared-down version, chicken legs roast first at high heat until they just begin to crisp. During the last 10 minutes of cooking, slices of oil-and-vinegar-soaked bread join the chicken on the sheet pan, where, together with the chicken, they bronze, the bread absorbing the released juices. Out of the oven, they rest, while a piquant dressing formulates on the sheet pan, the drippings liberated by a splash of oil and vinegar and the push of a wooden spoon. In the time it takes for the salad dressing to materialize, the chicken fully saturates the bread with its juices—roast chicken and *toast* salad in under an hour, a feat in its own right.

4 bone-in, skin-on chicken legs (7 to 8 ounces each)

6 tablespoons extra-virgin olive oil

Kosher salt and freshly cracked black pepper

4 tablespoons vinegar (white balsamic or red wine)

4 slices peasant bread (see page 22), ¾ inch thick

1 cup packed fresh basil or parsley leaves

2 garlic cloves

2 to 3 cups mixed green lettuces (5 ounces)

1. Place an oven rack in the top third of the oven and preheat it to 450°F. Place the chicken legs on a rimmed sheet pan. Pat the chicken very dry with paper towels, rub all over with 1 tablespoon oil, and season liberally with salt and pepper. Arrange the chicken, skin-side up, on the sheet pan, transfer to the oven, and roast for 30 minutes.

2. Meanwhile, in a 9 × 13-inch baking pan, whisk together 3 tablespoons oil with 2 tablespoons vinegar and a pinch of salt. Lay the bread into the pan, turning to coat so each slice evenly soaks up the dressing. When the chicken has roasted for 30 minutes, remove the sheet pan from the oven, add the soaked slices of bread to the pan around the chicken, reserving the 9 × 13-inch baking pan, and return the sheet pan to the oven for 10 minutes more, or until the bread is golden; check frequently during the last 2 to 3 minutes so the bread doesn't burn. Remove the sheet pan from the oven and transfer the chicken to a plate. Flip over the slices of bread and place them back in the oven for 3 to 5 minutes more, until they are deeply golden.

3. In the bowl of a food processor, blend the herbs, garlic, a pinch of salt, the remaining 2 tablespoons vinegar, and the remaining 2 tablespoons oil until smooth.

4. Remove the toasted bread from the sheet pan and tuck 1 slice under each leg of chicken resting on the plate. Immediately pour the herb sauce over the sheet pan, and scrape up the crispy bits with a wooden spoon. Transfer the bits and pan sauce to a small bowl. Place a toast-leg pair on each plate. Pour any juices from the chicken plate into the bowl with the sauce. Taste and adjust the seasoning as needed.

5. Using the reserved 9 × 13-inch baking pan, toss the salad greens lightly with some of the sauce. Taste and adjust the seasoning as needed. Pile a handful of greens onto each plate. Just before serving, spoon a little sauce over the chicken pieces.

SAVORY FRENCH TOAST
WITH THYME

SERVES 4 TO 6

For the same reason a chocolate chip cookie loves a sprinkling of salt or a slice of melon welcomes a blanket of prosciutto, custard-soaked bread brightens under a Parmigiano-Reggiano crust. These crisp-tender, thyme-scented toasts are all the more irresistible with a drizzle of maple syrup.

2 large eggs

1 cup 2 percent or whole milk

Pinch of kosher salt

1 tablespoon minced fresh thyme, plus more for garnish

6 slices day-old Soft Sandwich Bread (page 74), ¾ to 1 inch thick

1 cup freshly grated Parmigiano-Reggiano

Maple syrup, for serving

1. Place an oven rack about 4 inches from the broiler and preheat the broiler to high. In a 9 × 13-inch baking pan, whisk together the eggs, milk, salt, and 1 tablespoon thyme. Lay the slices of bread in the pan and let them sit for 5 minutes. Flip the slices and let them sit for another 5 minutes; almost all the custard should be absorbed by the end of the 10 minutes.

2. Place two cooling racks on a rimmed sheet pan. Lay the slices of bread on top of the racks. Scatter half the Parmigiano-Reggiano over the tops. Transfer to the oven and broil for 2½ to 3 minutes, until lightly golden, being sure to keep an eye on them during the final minutes so they don't burn. Using a spatula, flip the slices, sprinkle with the remaining cheese, and broil again for 2½ to 3 minutes more, until evenly golden and crispy.

3. Serve the French toast immediately garnished with more thyme on top and with syrup on the side.

BREAKFAST STRATA
WITH SAUSAGE, ONION, AND CHEDDAR

SERVES 4 TO 6

The basic ratio of a custard—1 egg to every ½ cup of milk or cream—is a handy one to memorize, an elemental concept I learned from Michael Ruhlman's *Ruhlman's Twenty*. This is the ratio used here and in every custard-based dish in this book: the sweet and savory French toasts (see pages 140 and 151), the bread puddings (see pages 210 and 236), the summer vegetable strata (see page 145), and the Fried Custard Cream (page 239). The beauty of understanding this concept is that, should you wish to scale this recipe up or down or choose to use an odd-size vessel, adjusting the quantity of eggs and milk is easy. Once you get the strata method down—line a pan with thin slices of bread, top with herbs, roasted vegetables, a little meat, and grated cheese, and pour custard over the top—you will never (*almost never*) need this recipe again.

1½ cups thinly sliced red onions
 (1 to 2 medium onions)

1½ cups finely chopped red or green bell pepper
 (about 1 large pepper)

2 tablespoons extra-virgin olive oil

1 teaspoon kosher salt, plus more as needed

Freshly cracked black pepper to taste

½ cup coarsely chopped fresh cilantro

⅓ cup finely chopped fresh chives

¼ pound hot Italian sausage, casing removed
 and crumbled

Softened unsalted butter, for greasing

5 to 6 slices day-old bread, such as Soft Sandwich
 Bread (page 74), peasant bread (see page 22), or
 Cheesy Cheddar and Parmigiano Bread (page 52),
 ½ inch thick, crusts removed

4 eggs

2 cups 2 percent or whole milk

1 cup (4 ounces) grated sharp Cheddar cheese

NOTE: The assembled strata can be refrigerated overnight for 8 to 10 hours. Bring it to room temperature before baking for about 50 minutes, or until lightly golden and firm to the touch. It saves and reheats well, too: cut the strata into 3-inch squares, place them on a sheet pan, and heat at 350°F for 15 minutes; the strata reheats nicely in the microwave as well.

1. Preheat the oven to 450°F. On a rimmed sheet pan, toss the onion and pepper with oil, ½ teaspoon salt, and pepper to taste. Arrange in an even layer, transfer to the oven, and roast for 10 minutes, or until the vegetables are soft and just beginning to color. Remove the pan from the oven and sprinkle with the cilantro and chives. Toss, taste, and adjust the seasoning with more salt or pepper to taste. Set aside.

2. Reduce the oven temperature to 350°F. In a small skillet over medium heat, brown the sausage until mostly cooked through, then remove the pan from the heat and set aside.

3. Lightly grease a 9-inch baking pan. Line the bottom of the pan with the slices of bread, tearing or using scraps to fill in the gaps, but do not overlap. Spoon the vegetables and any accumulated juices over the bread. Scatter the sausage evenly on top.

4. In a large bowl, beat the eggs with the milk and remaining ½ teaspoon salt until combined. Season with pepper to taste. Pour the mixture over the sausage, vegetables, and bread in the pan; the custard should just cover the contents of the pan. Top with the cheese.

5. Transfer the pan to the oven and bake for 35 minutes, or until lightly golden and firm to touch. Remove the pan from the oven and let it sit on a rack for 10 minutes before serving. Cut the strata into squares and serve it immediately.

SUMMER VEGETABLE STRATA
WITH GREEN PEPPER, CORN, AND ZUCCHINI

SERVES 6 TO 8

The virtues of a strata are endless: it's a no-fuss dish that feeds a crowd, it's well-suited for any time of day, and it's a format that can be adapted to whatever you have on hand. Vegetables benefit from a brief roasting first, but in a pinch, raw works fine. A little bit of meat—sausage, bacon, ham, pancetta—and a splash of Tabasco could transform this strata into a breakfast casserole. See the Note on page 142 for instructions on how to assemble it ahead of time and store it in the refrigerator.

1 small zucchini

1 heaping cup corn kernels, stripped from fresh ears (about 2)

1 cup thinly sliced red onion (about 1 small onion, halved and sliced)

1 green bell pepper, cut into ½-inch dice (about 1 cup)

2 tablespoons extra-virgin olive oil

1 teaspoon kosher salt

Freshly cracked black pepper to taste

Softened unsalted butter, for greasing

5 to 6 slices day-old bread, such as Soft Sandwich Bread (page 74), peasant bread (see page 22), or Cheesy Cheddar and Parmigiano Bread (page 52), ½ inch thick, crusts removed

⅓ cup chopped chives or scallions, white and green parts

½ cup fresh chopped basil

4 eggs

2 cups 2 percent or whole milk

Pinch of crushed red pepper flakes (optional)

1 cup (4 ounces) grated sharp Cheddar cheese

½ cup (2 ounces) crumbled feta

1. Preheat the oven to 450°F. Shred the zucchini on the large holes of a box grater; you should have 1½ to 2 cups. Squeeze the zucchini dry in a clean tea towel to remove moisture.

2. On a rimmed sheet pan, toss together the zucchini, corn, red onion, and bell pepper with the oil, ½ teaspoon salt, and black pepper to taste. Arrange them in an even layer, transfer the pan to the oven, and roast until the onion begins to turn golden, about 10 minutes. Remove the pan from the oven and set aside.

3. Reduce the oven to 350°F. Lightly grease a 9-inch baking pan. Line the bottom of the pan with the slices of bread, tearing or using scraps to fill in the gaps, but do not overlap. Spoon the roasted vegetables over the bread. Sprinkle the chives on top.

4. In a large bowl, beat the eggs with the milk and remaining ½ teaspoon salt until combined. Season with black pepper or red pepper flakes to taste, if desired. Pour the mixture over the bread and vegetables in the pan—the custard should just cover the contents of the pan. Top with both cheeses.

5. Transfer the pan to the oven and bake for 35 minutes, or until lightly golden and firm to the touch. Remove the pan from the oven and let the strata sit on a rack for 10 minutes before serving it. Cut the strata into squares and serve it immediately.

BEET-CURED SALMON
WITH HERBED CREAM CHEESE

SERVES 8 TO 10

When raw shredded beets top slabs of curing salmon, the rosy pigment bleeds out and permeates the fish, leaving an ombre stain across the glistening pink flesh. Black Seed Bagels in Manhattan popularized this breakfast treat, which is easy to replicate at home, requiring nothing more than time—the salmon takes 36 hours to cure—and a sharp knife. Served on homemade rye with a smear of herbed cream cheese, these toasts make a stunning brunch for a crowd.

1 side of salmon (2 to 2½ pounds), skin on
  (see Note)

⅔ cup kosher salt

½ cup sugar

¼ cup packed light or dark brown sugar

8 ounces beets, from 2 to 3 medium

2 loaves Rye Bread (page 48), sliced ¾ inch thick

Extra-virgin olive oil, for drizzling

Homemade Herbed Cream Cheese (recipe follows)
  or store-bought

Thinly sliced radishes, preferably watermelon
  radishes (optional), for serving

Lemon wedges (optional), for serving

NOTE: To create a silky-textured gravlax, a fatty piece of salmon is best. King salmon is the fattiest of the wild salmons, but it's incredibly expensive. Some fish markets and shops such as Whole Foods Market sell responsibly farmed salmon, whose relatively high fat content produces beautiful cured fish. A half recipe works well, too: for a 1-pound piece of salmon, use ⅓ cup salt, ¼ cup sugar, and 2 tablespoons brown sugar.

1. Place the salmon in the center of a rimmed sheet pan lined with parchment paper, foil, or plastic wrap. In a small bowl, combine the salt and sugars. Rub the mixture evenly over the surface of the salmon.

2. Grate the beets on a box grater or using the shredder attachment of a food processor. Scatter the beets evenly on top of the salmon. Cover the pan with another piece of parchment, foil, or plastic wrap, lay another sheet pan on top, and place the pan in the refrigerator. Place something heavy (like cans of tomatoes or a saucepan) on top of the upper sheet pan to weigh it down. Let it sit in the refrigerator for 36 hours.

3. Remove the pan from the refrigerator and scrape away the beets and discard them. Rinse off the salmon and pat it dry. Using your sharpest knife—a flexible fillet knife works well here—slice the salmon as thinly as possible.

4. To serve, preheat the oven to 425°F. Place the bread slices on a sheet pan and drizzle with oil. Toast until golden brown, 5 to 8 minutes. Remove the toasts from the oven and place them on a serving platter beside herbed cream cheese, slices of radishes (if using), lemon wedges (if using), and cured salmon.

Herbed Cream Cheese

MAKES 1½ CUP

1 cup cream cheese, room temperature

½ cup crème fraîche or sour cream

½ cup finely chopped fresh dill

4 tablespoons capers, rinsed, drained,
  and coarsely chopped

In the bowl of a stand mixer, whip the cream
cheese and crème fraîche together until light and
fluffy. Fold in the dill and capers using a spatula.
Chill, covered, until ready to use.

BROILED PEAR-FRANGIPANE TOASTS

SERVES 2

I have pastry chef David Lebovitz's *Room for Dessert* to thank for introducing me to frangipane, the almond-flavored cream used to enrich many French pastries, most especially the freeform fruit galette. An ode to those rustic tarts, these toasts celebrate that irresistible trinity of buttery dough, creamy almonds, and sweet fruit. Here, slices of pear sautéed briefly in butter fan the toasts, but any number of fruits could work: apples, plums, peaches, nectarines, or figs. Keep in mind that riper fruit will need less time in the sauté pan—a minute or two just to soften.

1 tablespoon unsalted butter

1 pear, peeled, cored, and thinly sliced

2 slices Soft Sandwich Bread (page 74) or
 Light Brioche (page 92), ¾ inch thick

2 tablespoons Frangipane (recipe follows)

1 teaspoon sugar

1. Preheat the broiler to high. In a large sauté pan over high heat, melt the butter. When it begins to bubble, add the pear slices and immediately reduce the heat to medium. Sauté, stirring occasionally, for 4 to 5 minutes, until the slices soften and the edges begin to brown. Remove the slices from the pan and set aside.

2. If the frangipane has been refrigerated, place it in a small bowl and beat it with a fork to soften; doing so allows for easier spreading. Place the bread slices on a cooling rack set on a rimmed sheet pan. Transfer them to the oven and broil for 2 minutes, or until lightly brown, keeping a close eye on them to prevent burning. Flip and spread each with about a tablespoon of frangipane. Layer the pear slices on top, being sure to cover the toast edge to edge. Sprinkle them evenly with sugar. Return them to the oven and broil them until caramelized, 2 to 3 minutes more.

3. Remove the pan from the oven and let the toasts cool briefly before serving them.

Frangipane

MAKES 1 CUP

1 scant cup almond flour or finely ground almonds
 (see Note)

¼ cup sugar

Pinch of kosher salt

4 tablespoons (½ stick) unsalted butter, softened

1 egg

1 tablespoon rum, brandy, bourbon,
 or vanilla extract (optional)

In the bowl of a stand mixer or food processor, combine the almond flour, sugar, salt, butter, and egg. Pulse until combined. Add the rum, if using, and pulse again until smooth. Transfer the frangipane to a storage container and chill until ready to use.

NOTE: If you can't find almond flour, you can pulse almonds (whole, sliced, slivered—whatever) in the food processor. The color of the frangipane will be brownish if you use almonds with skin, and the texture of the finished frangipane might not be as smooth, but the taste will still be great. The frangipane will keep in the refrigerator, covered, for up to 2 weeks.

BROILED FRENCH TOAST

SERVES 4 TO 6

The secret to former A Voce Columbus chef Filippo Gozzoli's French toast is confectioners' sugar, which he shakes heavy-handedly into the pan and onto each thick slice of brioche as it sears stovetop in clarified butter. His technique produces the most crispy-edged, creamy-centered, utterly delicious French toast imaginable. Here, use of the broiler allows us to use Gozzoli's technique to make French toast for a crowd. Be sure to watch the slices under the broiler closely—they can quickly turn from golden and caramelized to burnt and inedible.

2 large eggs

1 cup 2 percent or whole milk

1 tablespoon maple syrup, plus more for serving

1 tablespoon vanilla extract

¼ teaspoon kosher salt

6 slices day-old Light Brioche (page 92) or Soft Sandwich Bread (page 74), ¾ to 1 inch thick

½ cup confectioners' sugar

1. Place an oven rack 4 inches below the broiler and preheat the broiler to high. In a 9 × 13-inch baking dish, whisk together the eggs, milk, 1 tablespoon syrup, vanilla, and salt. Lay the slices of bread in the pan and let them sit for 5 minutes. Flip the slices and let them sit for another 5 minutes; almost all the custard should be absorbed at the end of the 10 minutes.

2. Line a sheet pan with two cooling racks. Lay the slices of bread on top of the racks. Sift half of the confectioners' sugar evenly over the top. Transfer the pan to the oven and broil the bread for 3 to 5 minutes, until lightly golden, being sure to keep an eye on them to prevent burning during the final minutes. Using a spatula, flip the slices, sprinkle them with the remaining confectioners' sugar, and broil them again for 3 to 5 minutes, until evenly golden and crispy.

3. Serve the French toast immediately with syrup alongside.

MASCARPONE AND SUGARED FRUIT TOASTS

SERVES 4

One of the simplest, most delicious desserts I've ever made comes from Gabrielle Hamilton's *Prune* and calls for toasting bread, buttering it, and topping it with sugared, sliced peaches. At the height of the summer, it makes an equally good breakfast. This toast pushes the recipe further along the dessert continuum by calling for brioche and a lightly sweetened, lemony mascarpone. If you want to take it one more step, broil the toasts until the mascarpone bubbles and the berries begin to burst. Or, if you have a hankering for it, try this recipe with Dark Chocolate Bread, which pairs particularly well with berries.

4 slices Light Brioche (page 92) or Dark Chocolate Bread (page 96), ¾ inch thick

¼ cup mascarpone cheese

1 tablespoons confectioners' sugar

Zest of 1 lemon

½ teaspoon vanilla extract

2 cups berries or sliced fruit (see Note)

Granulated sugar, for sprinkling

1. Toast the brioche in a toaster or under the broiler for 2 minutes per side, keeping a close watch—the sugar in the brioche causes it to brown quickly.

2. In a small bowl, beat the mascarpone with a fork to lighten it, then add the confectioners' sugar, zest, and vanilla. Spread a tablespoon of the mixture over each toast.

3. Top the toasts with a handful of berries or sliced fruit. Sprinkle them with sugar. Serve them immediately.

NOTE: Berries are particularly nice here, as are sliced stone fruit such as peaches, nectarines, and plums. Try whatever is in season and speaks to you.

GRILLED CHOCOLATE AND CRÈME FRAÎCHE SANDWICHES

SERVES 4

In an old *New York Times* article, Patricia Wells wrote about *le goûter de quatre heures*—snack time in France—a moment around four o'clock each afternoon when children's tummies begin to growl. When this witching hour strikes, parents and bakers across the country present treats often made with chocolate, such as *pain au chocolat* or *tartine au chocolat*, which Wells describes as thick slices of white bread, grilled over an open fire, spread with chilled crème fraîche and showered with grated dark chocolate. Can you imagine?

If you own a wood-burning oven, here's another reason to fire it up. If you don't, your skillet will do a fine job of lightly toasting the buttered bread and gently warming the whirl of chocolate and crème fraîche—the best antidote for the worst case of *les hangries*.

4 tablespoons (½ stick) unsalted butter, softened

2 tablespoons mayonnaise

8 slices Soft Sandwich Bread (page 74), ½ inch thick

¼ cup crème fraîche

1 tablespoon confectioners' sugar

Zest of ½ a lemon (about ½ teaspoon)

2 tablespoons plus 2 teaspoons chocolate-hazelnut spread, store-bought or homemade (see page 155)

1. In a medium bowl, beat the butter and mayonnaise together until well blended. Spread about 2 teaspoons of the mixture evenly, crust to crust, over each slice of bread. Lay them buttered-side down across a clean surface.

2. In a separate medium bowl, whisk together the crème fraîche, confectioners' sugar, and lemon zest. Spread about 2 teaspoons of this mixture over half of the unbuttered bread slices. Spread about 2 teaspoons of the chocolate-hazelnut spread over the remaining slices. Pair up the crème fraîche–slathered slices with the chocolate-slathered slices to make 4 sandwiches.

3. Set a griddle or large skillet over medium heat. Lay the sandwiches on the griddle or in the pan. Cook the bread until the undersides are golden, 2 to 3 minutes per side, checking after 1 minute to be sure they aren't too brown. Flip and cook the bread for another 2 minutes, or until they are golden. Remove the sandwiches from the griddle and let them rest 2 minutes before cutting and serving.

TOASTS
WITH BANANA AND CHOCOLATE-HAZELNUT SPREAD

SERVES 4; MAKES 1 CUP SPREAD

The only trouble with DIY pantry projects is that they make it hard to go back to the ready-made convenience items you always loved. Once you know that making almond butter (see page 117) requires nothing more than whizzing almonds until they liquefy, or that mayonnaise (see page 122) emulsifies in one minute, other store-bought items begin to lose their mystique, too. Here, roasted hazelnuts combine with cocoa to produce a homemade Nutella-like spread. It makes a lovely gift around the holidays but is a treat to have on hand year-round. These proportions produce a flavor geared more to the adult palate, but simply adjust the recipe with more confectioners' sugar if making it for children—or a grown-up with a very sweet tooth.

for the chocolate-hazelnut spread

1 cup hazelnuts (see Note)

¼ cup unsweetened cocoa, such as Hershey's Natural

½ cup confectioners' sugar, plus more as needed

¼ teaspoon kosher salt

2 to 3 tablespoons grapeseed or melted coconut oil, plus more as needed

1¼ teaspoons vanilla extract

for assembly

4 slices Light Brioche (page 92) or Soft Sandwich Bread (page 74), ¾ inch thick

2 bananas, sliced into ¼-inch-thick rounds

1. Make the chocolate-hazelnut spread: Preheat the oven to 350°F. Lay out the hazelnuts on a rimmed sheet pan, spreading them in a single layer. Toast them in the oven for 12 minutes, or until lightly golden. Remove the sheet pan from the oven. Transfer the nuts to a clean tea towel and rub them together to remove their skins. Let them cool completely, for about 10 minutes.

2. Transfer the nuts to the bowl of a food processor and purée them until they liquefy, about 6 minutes. Scrape down the sides of the bowl, then add cocoa, ½ cup confectioners' sugar, salt, 2 tablespoons oil, and vanilla. Pulse again until smooth. Taste and add more sugar as needed, or more oil to thin to the right consistency.

3. Transfer the chocolate-hazelnut spread to a glass jar and let it cool to room temperature. Store it at room temperature for up to 2 weeks.

4. Assemble the toasts: Toast the bread in a toaster or under the broiler, then lay them out on a clean surface. Spread each with about 2 teaspoons of the chocolate-hazelnut spread. Top with slices of banana and serve immediately.

NOTE: Almonds can be used in place of hazelnuts. If using almonds, there's no need to rub off their skins after toasting.

TOASTED BRIOCHE
WITH CARAMEL AND SEA SALT

SERVES 2; MAKES 1⅓ CUPS CARAMEL

When the elevenses strike, toasty brioche glistening with salted caramel comes to the rescue, each bite evoking Parisian café fare: plates of crepes and *pain perdu* drenched in puddles of *caramel au beurre salé*—it's fun to dream, right? Serve with a shot of espresso or strong coffee, a little bitterness to harness the sugar.

for the caramel

½ cup sugar

½ cup heavy cream, plus more for thinning

1 tablespoon unsalted butter

for assembly

2 slices Light Brioche (page 92), ¾ inch thick

Flaky sea salt, such as fleur de sel, for sprinkling

1. Make the caramel: Combine the sugar and 2 tablespoons water in a small, high-sided saucepan. Cook it over medium heat for about 5 minutes, or until the mixture turns amber, swirling the pan if necessary but resisting the urge to stir. Turn off the heat. Carefully add ½ cup cream—the mixture will bubble up—and stir with a heatproof spatula to incorporate. Add the butter and stir until melted. Let the caramel cool briefly, then transfer to a glass storage jar. It will thicken as it sits, and if it becomes too thick upon being stored, warm it again on the stovetop (or in the microwave), adding a little cream if necessary to achieve the desired consistency.

2. Assemble the brioche: Toast the slices of brioche in the toaster or under the broiler, keeping a close watch—the sugar in the brioche causes it to brown quickly.

3. Spread the slices of brioche with the caramel, sprinkle with sea salt, and serve them immediately.

ENGLISH SUMMER PUDDING

SERVES 6 TO 8

Sweet or savory, steamed or chilled, sticky or figgy—the British love their pudding. Summer pudding dates back to the 1800s and is as simple as it gets: day-old bread soaked with a mix of berries that have been cooked briefly with sugar to release their juices. After an overnight rest (or, at the very least, an eight-hour siesta) in the fridge, the juice of the berries stains the bread fuchsia. Served in bowls and drizzled with heavy cream, the white-to-purple contrast is striking, and the cool-on-cool combination refreshing. Kirsch, a clear liqueur distilled from cherries, is optional but will deepen the berry flavor without tasting boozy. Adding red or black currants to the mix of berries makes this especially traditional. With one bite you'll know: the proof is in the pudding.

½ cup sugar

Juice of ½ a lemon (about 4 teaspoons)

6 cups berries (I like a mix of raspberries, blueberries, and blackberries)

1 tablespoon kirsch (optional)

½ loaf Soft Sandwich Bread (page 74) or Light Brioche (page 92)

Heavy cream, for serving

1. In a large saucepan over low heat, melt the sugar with the lemon juice until the sugar has dissolved. Stir in the berries. Gently simmer for about 5 minutes, stirring every so often with a light touch, until the berries are soft but still whole. Add the kirsch, if using, then remove the pan from the heat and set aside.

2. Remove the crusts from the bread and cut it into ¼-inch-thick slices. Line an 8.5 × 4.5-inch loaf pan or 1-quart bowl with plastic wrap, then layer pieces of bread in it, overlapping the slices slightly to prevent gaps. Save some bread for the top.

3. Pour the berries and their juices into the bread-lined pan. Top with the reserved slices of bread. Cover the pan tightly with more plastic wrap, and set a heavy weight (such as a couple of cans of tomatoes) on top. If the pan is very full, place it on a rimmed sheet pan to catch any juices. Refrigerate it for at least 8 hours, and up to 24.

4. To serve, remove the pan from the refrigerator and unwrap the pudding. Working over the sink, place a large serving plate over the pudding and invert it, giving the vessel a little shake to release the pudding onto the plate. Peel away the remaining plastic wrap. Cut the pudding into slices, drizzle it with heavy cream, and serve immediately.

APPLE CHARLOTTE

SERVES 8 TO 10

Traditional apple charlotte calls for cooking apples down to a jam-like consistency, then packing the purée into a cylindrical mold lined with butter-soaked bread. Butter. Soaked. Bread. Yes, you read that correctly—now why don't we make charlottes more often? Here, vanilla permeates barely cooked apples, which meld into the buttery bread perimeter, which sops up slowly melting ice cream. It's an irresistible union made all the more enjoyable with a nip of Calvados or a shot of espresso. See the Note on page 47 for suggestions on types of apples.

2 pounds apples (3 to 4 apples), peeled, cored, and cut into ⅛-inch slices

2-inch piece of vanilla bean

10 tablespoons (1¼ sticks) unsalted butter

Pinch of kosher salt

½ cup sugar, plus more for sprinkling

2 tablespoons freshly squeezed lemon juice

½ loaf day-old Soft Sandwich Bread (page 74) or Light Brioche (page 92)

Vanilla ice cream, for serving

1. Set a rack in the middle of the oven and preheat it to 350°F. Place the apples in a large bowl and scrape in the vanilla bean seeds, reserving the pod.

2. In a large skillet, melt 2 tablespoons of the butter over low heat. Add the apples, a pinch of salt, and the vanilla bean pod. Stir, cover the pan, and cook for 15 minutes, or until the apples are soft but still have a little texture. Remove the pan from the burner and stir in ½ cup sugar and the lemon juice. Set aside.

3. Meanwhile, cut the bread into ½-inch-thick slices and remove the crusts. In a separate large skillet, melt the remaining 8 tablespoons of butter over low heat. Dip a slice of bread in the melted butter, then place it in a 4- or 6-cup ovenproof bowl or soufflé dish. Repeat with the remaining slices of bread until the bowl is lined. There is no need to overlap the bread—just cut it into wedges or other shapes as necessary to fit the odd gaps. The bread will meld together as it bakes.

4. Spoon the apples into the bowl right up to the top. Cover the top of the bowl with more slices of bread dipped in butter. Sprinkle sugar over the top.

5. Place the bowl on a sheet pan, transfer to the oven, and bake for 30 to 35 minutes, until the top and sides are golden. Remove the bowl from the oven and let the apple charlotte cool on a rack for 20 minutes.

6. To serve, spoon portions of the apple charlotte into bowls and top them with scoops of ice cream.

STRAWBERRY SHORTCAKE
WITH WHIPPED CREAM

SERVES 6 TO 8

When Buttermilk Pull-Apart Rolls are toasted briefly with melted butter, they can stand in for the traditionally called-for biscuits in strawberry shortcake. Sturdy yet squishy, filled with juicy berries and whipped cream, these stacks become dessert sliders, which are especially festive for the Fourth of July. Make them as soon as the strawberries start hitting the markets in late spring and early summer, and experiment with blueberries, raspberries, and blackberries all summer long.

for the strawberry shortcake

8 Buttermilk Pull-Apart Rolls (page 63) or biscuits

2 tablespoons (¼ stick) unsalted butter, melted

1 pound strawberries

1 tablespoon granulated sugar

for the whipped cream

½ cup heavy cream

1 to 2 tablespoons confectioners' sugar

½ teaspoon vanilla extract

1. Make the strawberry shortcake: Preheat the oven to 400°F. Separate the rolls and slice each in half crosswise. Place on a sheet pan, cut-side up, and evenly brush with the butter. Transfer to the oven and toast for about 10 minutes, or until lightly golden. Remove and transfer to a rack to cool briefly.

2. Meanwhile, stem and core the strawberries, then quarter them. Place in a large bowl and toss with the tablespoon of granulated sugar. Set aside.

3. Make the whipped cream: In the bowl of a stand mixer or using an electric mixer, beat together the cream and confectioners' sugar until soft peaks form. Add the vanilla and beat briefly to combine.

4. To assemble (see Note), place the bottom half of the rolls on a serving board. Mound the strawberries and their juices on top. Add big spoonfuls of the whipped cream and cover them with the top half of the rolls. Serve the strawberry shortcake immediately, passing around more whipped cream on the side.

NOTE: The strawberries and whipped cream can be prepared ahead, but the shortcakes should be assembled at the last minute.

CRUMBS

If I had to pick a transformative moment in the kitchen, it would be the first time I made eggs fried in bread crumbs from *The Zuni Café Cookbook*. The recipe calls for a mere three tablespoons of fresh bread crumbs, which get saturated in olive oil and heated in a skillet. Eggs then fry directly in these toasty crumbs, which encrust them in an irresistibly crispy shell. A sprinkling of vinegar, reduced in the pan, finishes it all off.

Before making these eggs, I had used dried bread crumbs for years, but never had I started from scratch with a slice of old bread and the food processor. Who knew that a handful of crumbs could so dramatically transform a dish? Well, as it turns out, many people do, generations of cooks who haven't been surrounded by the conveniences of today.

Limited by resources, cooks for centuries had to be creative with the humble ingredients they had on hand, and in the process, they created dishes and techniques we still celebrate today. It's hard now to look at a listless, crumbling slice of bread and not consider its future: crisped up and showered over pasta (see page 200), soaked in milk and mixed into meatballs (see page 229), saturated with oil and spread across a gratin (see page 195).

The recipes that follow call for both "big crumbs," torn or cubed bread fit for croutons (see page 182), bread puddings (see pages 210 and 236), panzanella salad (see page 169), fondue (see page 186), halloumi skewers (see page 173), and stuffing (see page 197), and "little crumbs," tiny crumbles of bread whose uses are vast, but which boil down to four general purposes:

AS A BREADING FOR MEAT, FISH, VEGETABLES, AND CHEESE. Many cuisines celebrate the cutlet, a thin piece of lean meat, pounded to ensure even, quick cooking, then breaded and often pan-fried. In Germany, it's *schnitzel;* in Japan, it's *tonkatsu;* in Italy, it's *una Milanese.* The typical breading procedure calls for dredging meat in flour, then egg, then dry bread crumbs (see page 178), but this process can be simplified. Often the three stations can be condensed into two by whisking flour and water in with the egg (see Crispy Goat Cheese Rounds with Shallot Vinaigrette, page 177), or the egg and flour can be replaced altogether with a spread such as mayonnaise or mustard (see Crispy Tarragon Cutlets, page 218, and Fish Sticks with Tartar Sauce, page 219).

AS A CRISPY GARNISH. In Italy it's called *pangrattato,* which translates to "grated bread," and in its simplest form that's all it is: day-old bread grated into crumbs and dried until crisp. But when the crumbs are crisped in some sort of fat (olive oil, butter, rendered bacon or pancetta fat, or schmaltz) and mixed with some sort of seasoning (herbs, zest, garlic, crushed red pepper flakes, spices, capers, or anchovies), they transform into irresistible morsels—also known as "poor man's Parmesan"—that can be showered on anything from salads to roasted vegetables to poached eggs. Once you learn the method—heat fat, add crumbs and seasonings, and cook until toasty (there, now you have)—you will never wonder what to make for dinner when the fridge is bare: crisp up bread crumbs with a few pantry items and toss them with hot pasta. Heaven.

AS A TOPPING. This is similar to *pangrattato*, but here the seasoned, moistened crumbs cook atop gratins, fish fillets, chicken legs, leftover beans, sautéed zucchini, and mac 'n' cheese. As the crumbs cook, they crisp into a thin layer, melding into whatever lies beneath them.

AS A THICKENER, BINDER, OR PANADE. Here's where crumbs get sneaky, adding body and texture, and thickening and binding whatever they are added to. In cuisines all over the world, bread plays an integral role in soups, with thick slices either set in soup bowls before the hot broth is ladled over or incorporated directly into the soup itself, where it breaks down into pieces, swells, and creates a porridge-like texture. Classic examples include Italian *pappa al pomodoro* (see page 185), Antonietta's Pancotto (page 217), *ribollita*, *acquacotta*, *minestra di pane*, and Spanish *ajo blanco* (see page 180), gazpacho, and *sopa de ajo*. A number of classic sauces, too, such as *picada* and *romesco*, rely on bread to provide body. In *skordalia*, a Greek condiment, bread binds the sauce just as it does in eggless Caesar dressing (see page 172). Bread crumbs have long been used to help fritters and veggie burgers (see page 211) hold their shape, and, of course, there is the *panade*, bread soaked in liquid, the secret to tender meatballs (see page 229) and meat loaves (see page 232).

PANZANELLA THREE WAYS

SERVES 4

If you are reading this book, chances are this statement speaks to you: the best way to eat a salad is to load it with carbohydrates. Tossed with juicy tomatoes, oily peppers, roasted vegetables, briny cheeses, fresh herbs, and tangy dressings, less-than-fresh bread revives—and the panzanella format is one of the best for using it up. On the following pages are three variations, but in the spirit of upcycling, improvise with what you have on hand—that's the real beauty of a good panzanella. Many of the loaves from the Bread chapter can be used in these three recipes, including peasant bread (see page 22), Three Seed Bread (page 28), Quinoa and Flax Bread (page 31), Roasted Garlic Bread (page 49), Walnut Bread (page 36), Cheesy Cheddar and Parmigiano Bread (page 52), and Potato Bread (page 53). If you are buying the bread rather than making it, look for a savory loaf without too many additional seasonings and without a thick, hard crust.

(recipe continues)

GREEK

2 tablespoons white balsamic vinegar

½ cup finely diced red onion (about 1 small onion)

½ teaspoon kosher salt, plus more as needed

Pinch of sugar

2 cups ¾-inch bread cubes (about 6 ounces)

⅓ cup plus 2 tablespoons extra-virgin olive oil

Freshly cracked black pepper to taste

2 cups halved cherry tomatoes or diced beefsteak tomatoes

1 cucumber (about 8 ounces), peeled, seeded, and cut into ½-inch dice (about 1 cup)

1 teaspoon Dijon mustard

½ cup crumbled feta, or more as needed

1. In a small bowl, pour the vinegar over the onion. Season with a pinch each of salt and sugar. Let stand for at least 15 minutes or up to a day.

2. Preheat the oven to 375°F. On a rimmed sheet pan, toss the bread cubes with 2 tablespoons oil. Season with ½ teaspoon salt and pepper to taste. Transfer to the oven and bake until golden brown and crunchy, about 10 minutes.

3. Transfer the bread cubes to a large bowl; add the tomatoes and cucumber. Add mustard and ⅓ cup oil to the bowl of macerating onions and whisk to combine. Pour the dressing over the bread and vegetables and toss to coat. Season with more pepper to taste.

4. Gently toss in the feta and serve.

NOTE: Kalamata Olive Bread (page 44) or Rosemary Semolina Bread with Pine Nuts (page 29) would also be nice here.

ROASTED RED PEPPERS AND FOCACCIA

2 pounds red bell peppers, seeded and cut into 1-inch slices

Kosher salt and freshly cracked black pepper to taste

6 tablespoons extra-virgin olive oil

3 cups ¾-inch-cubed focaccia (page 69), (about 6 ounces) (see Note)

¼ cup toasted pine nuts (see Note, page 114)

1 cup diced fresh mozzarella

1 tablespoon capers

½ cup roughly chopped fresh basil

1 tablespoon vinegar (white balsamic, balsamic, or red wine)

1. Preheat the oven to 450°F. In a large bowl, season the bell peppers with salt and pepper to taste. Drizzle with 2 tablespoons of the oil and toss to coat. Arrange them, skin-side down, on a sheet pan. Transfer to the oven and roast for 25 to 30 minutes, until the peppers are tender and slightly browned on the edges; thinner peppers will cook more quickly, so start checking them at 20 to 25 minutes. Remove the peppers and set them aside to cool. Reduce the oven temperature to 375°F.

2. Toss the focaccia cubes with 2 tablespoons oil on a rimmed sheet pan. Season lightly with salt and pepper to taste. Bake until golden brown and crunchy, 8 to 10 minutes.

3. In a large bowl, toss together the toasted bread, pine nuts, peppers, mozzarella, capers, basil, remaining 2 tablespoons oil, vinegar, and salt and pepper to taste. Taste and adjust seasoning as needed.

WINTER PANZANELLA WITH YOGURT-TAHINI DRESSING

1 small butternut squash (1½ to 2 pounds), cut into ¾-inch pieces

2 medium red onions, cut into ½-inch wedges

5 tablespoons extra-virgin olive oil

Kosher salt and freshly cracked black pepper to taste

2 cups ¾-inch bread cubes (about 6 ounces)

2 tablespoons vinegar (white balsamic, balsamic, or red wine)

⅓ cup pomegranate seeds

⅓ cup Yogurt-Tahini Dressing (recipe follows), plus more to taste

1. Preheat the oven to 450°F. On a sheet pan, toss the squash and onion wedges with 2 tablespoons oil, a generous pinch of salt, and pepper to taste. Arrange them in an even layer, transfer to the oven, and roast for 20 to 22 minutes, until the edges of the vegetables are just beginning to brown.

2. Meanwhile, in a large bowl, toss the bread cubes with the remaining 3 tablespoons oil, vinegar, and salt and pepper to taste. Add them to the sheet pan with the vegetables after the 20 to 22 minutes, and toss them to coat. Return the pan to the oven and toast the bread for 6 to 8 minutes more, until it is golden.

3. Remove the pan from the oven and spread the vegetables and bread cubes onto a large serving platter. Scatter the pomegranate seeds on top, drizzle with the yogurt-tahini dressing, and serve with more dressing on the side.

Yogurt-Tahini Dressing

MAKES 1 CUP

¼ cup well-stirred tahini paste

⅓ cup plain full-fat yogurt

2 to 3 tablespoons fresh lemon juice

1 small garlic clove, minced (optional)

¼ to ½ teaspoon kosher salt

1 teaspoon maple syrup

In a medium bowl, combine the tahini, yogurt, 2 tablespoons of the lemon juice, the garlic, if using, ¼ teaspoon of the salt, maple syrup, and 2 tablespoons water. Taste and add more lemon and salt as needed. Thin the dressing with water, a teaspoon at a time, until it reaches a pourable consistency.

KALE CAESAR SALAD
WITH EGGLESS DRESSING

SERVES 3 TO 4 AS A SIDE DISH

Just as crumbs are used to thicken soups and sauces, they also do the same brilliantly for salad dressings. Without mayonnaise or egg yolks for emulsification, bread crumbs, water, vinegar, and oil can blend into a thick, creamy dressing. This technique, which has been featured on Food52's Genius Recipes column, has long been used in sauces such as *bagnet vert*, an Italian condiment, and *skordalia*, a Greek dipping sauce often served with fried fish and vegetables. Here it has been applied to make an egg-free Caesar dressing fit for any salad that's destined to bask on the buffet for hours. A blender works best to whip in air, though a food processor will do the trick, too.

for the dressing

1 large garlic clove

2 anchovies

2 tablespoons vinegar (white balsamic, white wine, or red wine)

1 teaspoon sugar

¾ cup fresh bread crumbs (see Note)

⅓ cup extra-virgin olive oil

Kosher salt and freshly cracked black pepper to taste

for the salad

1 cup walnuts

½ pound Tuscan kale, rough ends trimmed, cut into thin ribbons

1 to 2 tablespoons vinegar (white balsamic, white wine, or red wine)

½ cup grated Parmigiano-Reggiano

1. Make the dressing: Place the garlic, anchovies, vinegar, and sugar in a blender. Pulse until smooth. Add the bread crumbs and 2 tablespoons water and pulse again to combine. Scrape down the sides, then let the mixture sit untouched for 5 minutes to allow the bread to absorb the liquid.

2. With the motor running, drizzle in the oil and blend until the mixture is thick and smooth. Once thickened, drizzle in water, 1 tablespoon at a time (with the motor still running), until the dressing reaches a thick but pourable consistency. Taste and add salt and pepper as needed.

3. Make the salad: In a small sauté pan, toast the walnuts over medium heat until lightly browned and fragrant, about 10 minutes. Transfer to a clean tea towel and rub to remove the papery skins. Transfer to a sieve and shake to remove any additional skins.

4. In a large bowl, toss the kale with dressing to coat. Taste and add vinegar as needed. Add the walnuts and Parmesan and toss again. Let the salad sit for 5 minutes to allow the kale to soften. Taste and adjust the seasoning with salt, pepper, and more vinegar.

NOTE: Fresh bread crumbs sounds like an oxymoron—but it just means not dried. To make them, simply pulse bread, preferably at least one day old, in a food processor until roughly the size of peppercorns. If you are using bread with thick crusts, remove them before pulsing—the crust of the peasant bread (see page 22), however, does not need to be removed. Dried bread crumbs or panko should not be used in place of fresh—they will not absorb flavor as well, and, moreover, they will get overtoasted when they are crisped with oil or butter.

HALLOUMI AND BREAD SKEWERS
WITH BAGNA CAUDA

SERVES 4 AS AN APPETIZER

Every few years for Easter, my Greek family goes all out, roasting a whole lamb on a spit over an outdoor fire pit. Just as enjoyable as the finished meat itself are the treats we consume throughout the day as it cooks: bread rubbed along the bronzing body, salty halloumi grilled below that is soaked with the lamb's juices. In place of spit-roasted lamb juices, these skewers, an ode to my family's rituals, are brushed with *bagna cauda*, a classic Italian dip—a warm anchovy-and-butter bath—typically served with vegetables but also with *spiedini di mozzarella* (skewers of mozzarella and bread). These are perfect party fare. Be sure to serve the extra *bagna cauda* and bread on the side.

for the bagna cauda

2 cloves garlic, minced

2 anchovies, minced

4 tablespoons (½ stick) unsalted butter

4 tablespoons extra-virgin olive oil

for the skewers

8 ounces halloumi cheese, cut into 1-inch cubes

4 cups 1-inch cubes of bread, such as peasant bread (see page 22), Quinoa and Flax Bread (page 31), or Rosemary Semolina Bread with Pine Nuts (page 29)

1 teaspoon neutral oil

Fresh lemon wedges, for serving

1. Make the bagna cauda: In a small skillet over medium heat, combine the garlic, anchovies, butter, and oil. Cook until the butter melts and the mixture just begins to bubble, about 5 minutes. Remove the pan from the heat and set aside.

2. Make the skewers: Thread the bread and cheese onto the skewers, alternating as you spear, so they hold 2 pieces of each. Brush all around with the bagna cauda.

3. Preheat a grill or grill pan to high. When it begins to smoke, brush it with the teaspoon of oil, then wipe it away. Reduce the heat to medium-high. Place the skewers on the grill or grill pan and cook for 2 minutes per side, or until the cheese forms a nice golden crust and the bread is toasty.

4. Remove the skewers from the grill and transfer them to a platter. Serve them with lemon wedges and the remaining bagna cauda on the side.

HEARTS OF ROMAINE
WITH BACON CRUMBS
AND BLUE CHEESE-BUTTERMILK DRESSING

SERVES 4

In this iteration of the classic 1940s wedge salad, hearts of romaine, quartered to expose their web of crevices, catch and cradle bits of bacon and bread crumbs crisped in rendered bacon fat. Dressed in a tangy blue cheese–buttermilk dressing, the sturdy green holds up well, allowing the salad to be assembled ahead of time. Make it at the height of the summer—crisp and cool have never tasted better.

3 slices bacon, finely diced

⅓ cup fresh bread crumbs (see Note, page 172)

4 small heads romaine lettuce

1 pint cherry tomatoes, halved

Sea salt and freshly cracked black pepper to taste

¼ cup Blue Cheese Dressing (recipe follows), plus more as needed

1. In a medium skillet, cook the bacon over medium heat until the fat is rendered and the bacon is crisp, 8 to 10 minutes. Transfer the bacon to a paper-towel-lined plate to drain, leaving the fat behind—there should be about 1 tablespoon. Add the bread crumbs to the pan and cook until golden and crisp, 5 to 10 minutes, reducing the heat as necessary to prevent burning. Transfer the crumbs to the plate with the bacon.

2. Trim any dark, wilted green ends off the tops of the romaine heads. Halve through the core, keeping the core intact. Halve each half again. Arrange the wedges on a large serving platter.

3. Scatter the cherry tomatoes over and all around the wedges. Season everything lightly with salt and pepper to taste.

4. Use a spoon to drizzle the dressing over the lettuce and tomatoes. Scatter the bacon–bread crumb mixture over the top and serve.

Blue Cheese Dressing

MAKES 1 CUP

4 ounces blue cheese, such as Gorgonzola

1 tablespoon white balsamic vinegar, plus more as needed

¼ cup crème fraîche or sour cream

2 tablespoons buttermilk, plus more as needed

Kosher salt and freshly cracked black pepper to taste

1. Combine the cheese, vinegar, crème fraîche, and 2 tablespoons buttermilk in a blender or food processor. Season with salt and pepper. Pulse until smooth. Taste and adjust the seasonings as needed, adding more buttermilk, 1 tablespoon at a time, to thin the dressing to the right consistency, if necessary.

2. Add a splash of vinegar for more bite, if desired.

CRISPY GOAT CHEESE ROUNDS
WITH SHALLOT VINAIGRETTE

MAKES 6 ROUNDS

For years, limited counter space deterred me from breading anything. But when a friend taught me that the three-step coating process often can be turned into two simply by whisking the egg *with* a little flour and water, a world of breaded foods became my oyster, most especially these delicious goat cheese rounds—salad's favorite garnish! Piled on a bed of greens, these rounds make a nice appetizer or first course, but for a savory-sweet dessert, drizzle with honey or serve with a fruity compote.

2 tablespoons finely minced shallots

2 tablespoons white balsamic vinegar,
 plus more as needed

Kosher salt

Pinch of freshly cracked black pepper

Pinch of sugar

8-ounce log of goat cheese, cut into six ¾-inch slices

1 large egg

2 tablespoons unbleached all-purpose flour

¾ cup Homemade Dried Bread Crumbs
 (recipe follows) or panko

Neutral oil, for frying

Flaky sea salt, for finishing

⅓ cup extra-virgin olive oil, plus more as needed

5 ounces (about 8 cups) salad greens

2 beefsteak or heirloom tomatoes, sliced

1. In a medium bowl, place the shallots and cover them with the vinegar. Season with a pinch each of salt, pepper, and sugar. Set aside to macerate for at least 10 minutes.

2. Meanwhile, slightly flatten each goat cheese round to a ½-inch thickness.

3. In a shallow medium bowl, whisk the egg with the flour, 1 tablespoon water, and a pinch of salt. Place the crumbs in a shallow, rimmed dish, such as a small sheet pan. Dip a goat cheese round in the egg mixture, allowing any excess to drip off, then into the bread crumbs, pressing them to adhere. Repeat with the remaining rounds.

4. Heat a thin layer of neutral oil in a large sauté pan over medium heat. When it begins to shimmer, gently place the breaded rounds in the sauté pan—they should sizzle on contact. Immediately reduce the heat to low. After 1 to 2 minutes, when the rounds begin to brown on the bottom, flip each and brown the other side. Cook 1 to 2 minutes more, then use a spatula to remove each to a clean paper-towel-lined plate. Sprinkle lightly with sea salt.

5. Whisk the olive oil into the macerated shallots. Taste and adjust the seasoning with more salt, vinegar, or oil as needed. Toss the greens and tomatoes with the dressing. Arrange them on a platter beside the crispy goat cheese rounds.

NOTE: Breaded rounds can be chilled in the refrigerator in an airtight container for as long as 24 hours.

(recipe continues)

Homemade Dried Bread Crumbs

If you are using bread with an especially thick crust, remove it before proceeding with this recipe. If you're making crumbs with the Peasant Bread Master Recipe (page 22), there is no need to remove the crusts, though if you would like to make especially light, panko-style crumbs, do so as well before proceeding with the instructions.

Slow Method

Preheat the oven to 250°F. Pulse the bread in a food processor until fine, like the texture of coarse polenta. Spread the crumbs on a sheet pan, transfer the pan to the oven, and toast the crumbs until very dry, 45 to 60 minutes; the crumbs should take on very little color. Remove the pan from the oven and let it cool completely. If you want finer crumbs, return them to the food processor and pulse to reach your desired texture. Store the bread crumbs in an airtight container at room temperature for up to 2 months.

Fast Method

Preheat the oven to 375°F. Pulse the bread in a food processor until fine. Spread the crumbs on a sheet pan, transfer the pan to the oven, and toast the crumbs for 10 to 15 minutes, until evenly golden. Remove the pan from the oven and let it cool completely. If you want finer crumbs, return them to the food processor and pulse to reach the desired texture. Store the bread crumbs in an airtight container at room temperature for up to 2 months.

GREEN GAZPACHO
WITH TOMATO SALSA

SERVES 4

Ajo blanco, also known as white gazpacho, is a chilled summer soup originally from Andalusia. Arabs, who ruled the Iberian Peninsula for centuries, brought almonds to the region and are believed to have introduced this soup as well, which is typically made with almonds, bread, and garlic. Green grapes are a usual garnish, a sweet counterpoint to the bracing purée, but here they join the mix, along with cucumber and fresh dill, all of which tinge the soup a light green. Topped with a spicy tomato salsa, this striking soup is a nice addition to a summer lunch or dinner.

for the gazpacho

1 English cucumber (about 12 ounces), thinly sliced

½ pound seedless green grapes, halved

1 garlic clove, minced

1 teaspoon kosher salt, plus more as needed

¼ cup white balsamic vinegar

2 slices of peasant bread (see page 22) or Soft Sandwich Bread (page 74), cut ½ inch thick and torn into pieces

¼ cup almonds

¼ cup fresh dill leaves

2 tablespoons extra-virgin olive oil

⅓ to ½ cup plain whole milk yogurt

Freshly cracked black pepper to taste

for the tomato salsa

1¼ cups cherry tomatoes, quartered

½ cup finely diced red onion

1 jalapeño, finely minced (about 1 tablespoon) (see Note)

Pinch of kosher salt

2 tablespoons extra-virgin oil

1 tablespoon white balsamic vinegar, plus more as needed

1. Make the gazpacho: In a large bowl, combine the cucumber, grapes, and garlic. Add 1 teaspoon of salt and the vinegar, toss to coat, and set aside to marinate for 20 minutes.

2. Meanwhile, in a small bowl, pour ⅓ cup water over the bread. Let it sit until it softens, about 10 minutes.

3. In a small skillet over medium heat, toast the almonds, tossing frequently, until fragrant and starting to color, about 5 minutes. Immediately transfer to a plate to cool, about 5 minutes.

4. Add the almonds to a food processor and pulse until finely minced. Add the cucumber mixture, soaked bread and liquid, dill, oil, yogurt, and a grinding of black pepper to the processor bowl. Purée until smooth. Season to taste with salt and pepper. Chill until ready to serve.

5. Make the tomato salsa: In a medium bowl, combine the tomatoes, onion, jalapeño, salt, oil, and vinegar. Taste and adjust seasoning as needed with more salt and/or vinegar.

6. To serve, ladle the soup into bowls. Spoon a tablespoon of the salsa over each bowl of soup just before serving, passing more on the side.

NOTE: Seed the jalapeños before mincing them if you are sensitive to heat.

ESCAROLE-LEEK SOUP
WITH GREMOLATA CROUTONS

SERVES 4

Here, butter-roasted croutons are showered with the Italian condiment *gremolata*, a mixture of parsley, garlic, and lemon zest that classically is served with braised veal. When floated atop a wintry escarole and leek soup, these croutons brighten the flavors and provide texture to every spoonful. If you are a fan of Italian wedding soup, serve this dish with Pan-Fried Turkey Meatballs (page 231). Two tips: Zest the lemon before juicing it! You'll need the former for the croutons and the latter for the soup. And while you can save your own, of course, many grocery stores now sell rinds of Parmigiano-Reggiano, which add tremendous flavor to soups and stews. Wrapped in an airtight bag, these rinds can be frozen for months.

for the gremolata croutons

2 cups ½-inch-cubed bread such as peasant bread (see page 22), Roasted Garlic Bread (page 49), Cheesy Cheddar and Parmigiano Bread (page 52), or Potato Bread (page 53)

2 to 3 tablespoons unsalted butter, melted

Sea salt and freshly cracked black pepper to taste

1 garlic clove, minced

2 tablespoons finely minced fresh parsley

Zest of 1 lemon

for the soup

4 cups thinly sliced leeks, soaked and drained (see Note)

2 tablespoons extra-virgin olive oil

2 tablespoons (¼ stick) unsalted butter

¾ pound escarole, base removed, chopped into 2-inch pieces (about 12 cups), soaked and drained (see Note)

Kosher salt and freshly cracked black pepper to taste

4 to 5 cups homemade Chicken Stock (recipe follows) or store-bought

2-inch piece of Parmigiano-Reggiano rind (optional)

Juice of ½ a lemon, plus more as needed

1 cup grated Parmigiano-Reggiano

NOTE: To clean and prepare the leeks, trim off and discard the root and the leafy dark green top. Cut the leek in half lengthwise, then slice into thin half-moons. Place the leeks in a large bowl. Cover the leeks with cold water, separating the slices, and let them sit for 5 minutes to allow any dirt to settle to the bottom of the bowl. After 5 minutes, use your hands or a slotted spoon to lift the leeks out of the water, leaving the grit and dirt behind; a little water clinging to the leeks is fine. This technique applies to escarole as well.

1. Make the gremolata croutons: Preheat the oven to 375°F. On a sheet pan, toss the bread cubes with 1 tablespoon of melted butter. Season with salt and pepper to taste. Transfer to the oven and toast for 8 to 10 minutes, until golden.

2. Remove the croutons from the oven and transfer to a large bowl. Add 1 more tablespoon melted butter, the minced garlic, parsley, and lemon zest. Toss to coat evenly with the seasonings; the seasonings will not adhere completely to the croutons. Taste and add more salt and pepper, if necessary. Add the remaining tablespoon of butter, if desired. Croutons can be made several hours in advance and stored at room temperature.

3. Make the soup: In a large stockpot over medium heat, place the leeks, oil, and butter, and stir to coat. When the leeks begin to sizzle, reduce the heat to medium-low and sauté until golden and soft, about 10 minutes.

4. Add the escarole, cover the pot, and reduce the heat to low. Simmer until the escarole wilts, about 5 minutes. Sprinkle the greens with a generous pinch of salt and some pepper.

5. Add the stock and the cheese rind, if using. Increase the heat to high and bring the soup to a boil, then reduce the heat to medium-low and simmer for 10 minutes to allow the flavors to meld. Add the juice from half a lemon. Taste and adjust the seasoning with more lemon, salt, and pepper as needed.

6. To serve, ladle piping-hot soup into bowls. Sprinkle each bowl generously with cheese and top with a small handful of croutons.

Chicken Stock

MAKES 1½ QUARTS

3 pounds chicken pieces, such as wings or legs

2 stalks celery

2 carrots

½ teaspoon whole black peppercorns

1 bay leaf

1 onion, cut in half

1 teaspoon kosher salt

1. Place all the ingredients in a large pot and cover with cold water. Bring to a boil over high heat, then reduce the heat to low and simmer for 2 to 3 hours, until the stock tastes flavorful. Let it cool with the bones and vegetables in the pot. Remove the bones and strain the stock into a clean pot or bowl.

2. Refrigerate the stock overnight, then skim off the fat, which will have risen to the top and hardened. Store the stock in the freezer for up to 3 months.

ROASTED TOMATO AND BREAD SOUP

Traditional *pappa al pomodoro* (tomato and bread soup) is made with the ripest tomatoes and yesterday's bread. Here, slow-roasting the tomatoes with carrots, garlic, and onions at a low temperature deepens their flavor. Water reconstitutes the super-concentrated vegetables into an ultra-flavorful soup, and dry bread, swelling as it sits, gives body to this Tuscan comfort dish. Just before serving, shave Parmigiano-Reggiano on top and drizzle with olive oil or swirl in toasted Bread-Crumb Chimichurri (page 225).

4 pounds (4 to 5 medium beefsteak) tomatoes, halved

1¼ pounds (2 medium) onions, chopped

1 head garlic, cloves separated and peeled

4 ounces (2 large) carrots, unpeeled and roughly chopped

¼ cup extra-virgin olive oil, plus more for drizzling (optional)

1 teaspoon kosher salt, plus more as needed

Freshly cracked black pepper to taste

2 slices peasant bread (see page 22), ½ inch thick

Crushed red pepper flakes to taste (optional)

1 bunch fresh basil leaves

Shaved Parmigiano-Reggiano, for serving (optional)

1. Preheat the oven to 300°F. Arrange the tomatoes, onions, garlic cloves, and carrots on a rimmed sheet pan in an even layer. Drizzle with ¼ cup oil and season with 1 teaspoon kosher salt and pepper to taste. Transfer to the oven and roast for 2½ to 3 hours, until the vegetables are soft and slightly caramelized.

2. About 20 minutes before the vegetables should be finished, stick the bread directly on the oven racks to roast alongside the sheet pan—you want to dry out the bread, not brown it. Remove the sheet pan and the bread from the oven.

3. In a large pot over medium heat, place the vegetables and 2½ cups water. Slowly bring the soup to a simmer to prevent bubbling and splattering.

4. Season the vegetables with a pinch of salt and crushed red pepper flakes, if using. Add the basil. Break 1 slice of bread into medium-size pieces and add it to the pot. Using an immersion blender, food processor, or traditional blender, roughly purée the soup—it should be slightly chunky. Crumble in the other slice of bread and roughly purée or thin with 1 tablespoon water at a time to reach your desired consistency. Taste and add more salt as needed.

5. To serve, ladle the soup into bowls and top each with a drizzle of oil and a few shavings of Parmigiano-Reggiano, if desired.

CLASSIC FONDUE

SERVES 4

From *queso fundido* to baked fontina, it's hard to find fault in a vat of warm, silky cheese. Few genres of food more quickly summon the masses and better promote communal eating, fondue being no exception. Making fondue couldn't be simpler—heat wine, melt cheese—though it is imperative to use cornstarch to allow the two ingredients to blend into a unified sauce. And although a splash of kirsch—a clear brandy distilled from cherries—is traditional, it certainly can be left out.

1 pound Gruyère or Comté cheese, grated (see Note, page 55)

8 ounces Emmental cheese, grated (see Note, page 55)

2 tablespoons cornstarch

½ garlic clove

1½ cups white wine

2 tablespoons lemon juice

Grating of fresh nutmeg (optional)

1 to 2 teaspoons kirsch (optional)

1 loaf peasant bread (see page 22), cut into 1-inch cubes, for serving

Cornichons or other pickles, for serving

Cured meats, for serving

1. In a large bowl, toss the cheeses together with the cornstarch.

2. Rub the bottom of a large, wide pot with the garlic. Add the wine and bring it to a gentle simmer over medium-high heat.

3. Add one-third of the cheese mixture and stir it to melt. Add another third and stir to melt. Add the remaining cheese and stir until blended.

4. Stir in the lemon juice. Shave fresh nutmeg on top, if using, and taste. Add 1 teaspoon kirsch, if using, and stir it to combine. Taste and adjust the seasoning as needed. Serve the fondue immediately with cubed bread, cornichons, and meats.

PAN-STEAMED CAULIFLOWER
WITH ANCHOVY-CAPER CRUMBS

SERVES 3 TO 4

As cauliflower cooks, it sweetens and welcomes sharp, salty dressings. Here, it is steamed until knife-tender in a mixture infused with anchovies and garlic before it meets a showering of capered bread crumbs. A briny sauce materializes during the steaming, which easily allows this simple side dish to become a meal: simply toss it with cooked pasta. A pinch of crushed red pepper flakes and a few shavings of Parmigiano-Reggiano would be welcome additions.

4 tablespoons (½ stick) unsalted butter

2 garlic cloves, minced

2 to 3 anchovies, minced to yield about 1 teaspoon

2 pounds cauliflower, cut into florets (about 7 cups)

Kosher salt and freshly cracked black pepper to taste

½ cup fresh bread crumbs (see Note, page 172)

1 tablespoon capers

1. In a large, wide pot, combine 3 tablespoons butter, 3 tablespoons water, minced garlic, and anchovies over medium heat. Add the cauliflower and season with a pinch of salt and pepper to taste. Bring the liquid to a boil, cover, then immediately reduce the heat to medium-low. Steam without touching the pot for 10 minutes, then remove the lid and stir—add another tablespoon of water if the liquid has nearly evaporated. Re-cover and cook for 5 to 10 minutes more, until cauliflower is knife-tender.

2. Meanwhile, in a medium sauté pan over medium heat, toast the bread crumbs for 5 to 7 minutes, until golden, then transfer them to a plate. Immediately add the remaining 1 tablespoon butter and capers to the same pan and cook until the capers burst open, 1 to 2 minutes. Return the bread crumbs to the pan and stir to coat. Remove the pan from the heat and set aside.

3. Transfer the cauliflower to a large serving platter, being sure to pour the juices from the pot over the top. Toss the cauliflower to coat. Taste and season it with more salt and pepper, if necessary. Scatter the crumbs on top of the cauliflower and serve.

SPICY BROCCOLI SAUTÉ

SERVES 4

Here's a mantra to keep in mind whenever your side-dish game is in need of a boost: toasty bread crumbs and spicy garlic-infused oil. The key here is to cook the broccoli just until the spears are knife-tender, as they continue to cook when they sauté with the spicy, garlicky oil. Cauliflower, green beans, asparagus, and snap peas all take well to this same treatment.

¼ cup plus 1 tablespoon extra-virgin olive oil

½ cup fresh bread crumbs (see Note, page 172)

Sea salt

½ teaspoon crushed red pepper flakes

4 garlic cloves, thinly sliced

2 pounds broccoli, cut into spears (6 to 7 cups)

1. Bring a large pot of water to a boil over high heat. Meanwhile, in a large sauté pan, heat 1 tablespoon of the oil over medium heat. When it begins to shimmer, add the bread crumbs and a pinch of salt, and sauté until golden and crisp, stirring occasionally, about 5 minutes. Transfer to a plate to cool.

2. Wipe the pan clean and add the remaining oil, pepper flakes, and garlic. Heat just until the garlic begins to sizzle, 1 to 2 minutes, then remove the pan from the heat and set aside.

3. When the water is boiling, add the broccoli and cook until knife-tender, 3 to 5 minutes, depending on the size of the spears. Drain.

4. Reheat the garlicky oil over medium-high heat until the garlic begins to sizzle, 2 to 3 minutes. Add the broccoli, season with a pinch of salt, and cook for 30 seconds, tossing to coat. Transfer the broccoli to a platter, sprinkle it with the crumbs, and serve it immediately.

SAUTÉED GREENS
WITH LEMON-PARSLEY CRUMBS AND POACHED EGG

SERVES 2

In early summer, when the greens from my farm share arrive in droves, this simple formula makes near-daily appearances: sautéed greens + poached egg + crispy bread crumbs. It works equally well with chard, mustard greens, and tender kale as with beet, turnip, radish, or any other root greens that may otherwise be neglected in the vegetable bin. Once the bread crumbs are toasted, this whole dish comes together in less than 5 minutes: As the eggs poach in their covered pot, the greens shrink to half their size. A splash of vinegar, reduced quickly, completes the dressing, priming the greens for the rich yolk and bright, lemony crumbs.

3 tablespoons extra-virgin olive oil

⅓ cup fresh bread crumbs (see Note, page 172)

Kosher salt and freshly cracked black pepper

Zest of 1 lemon

1 tablespoon finely chopped fresh parsley

8 cups (5 ounces) greens, such as mustard, beet, turnip, or spinach

2 eggs

Pinch of crushed red pepper flakes

2 teaspoons vinegar (red wine, white wine, or white balsamic), plus more as needed

1. Bring a small pot of water to a boil over high heat. Meanwhile, in a large sauté pan, heat 1 tablespoon of the oil over medium heat. When it begins to shimmer, add the crumbs and toast until golden and crisp, about 5 minutes. Season with a pinch of salt and pepper, and transfer to a plate to cool. Add the zest and parsley and toss gently to combine. Wipe the pan clean and set it aside.

2. Place the greens in a colander, run them under cold water, and set them aside to drain. Shake the colander to remove excess water, though a little bit of water clinging to the greens is fine.

3. Crack each egg into its own small ramekin or bowl for easy transfer. When the small pot of water is boiling, turn off the heat. Slide the eggs into the pot, cover, and let stand for 4 to 5 minutes, or until the whites are set and the yolks are still soft—lift one egg from the water with a slotted spoon and shake it gently to test. Remove the eggs with a slotted spoon and transfer them to a paper-towel-lined plate to drain.

4. Meanwhile, in the large sauté pan used for the crumbs, heat the remaining 2 tablespoons of oil over high heat. When the oil begins to shimmer, add a pinch of pepper flakes followed immediately by the greens—be careful: the oil may splatter if the greens are too wet. Season with a pinch of salt and cook undisturbed for 1 minute, then use tongs to stir and rearrange the greens until they are completely wilted, about 1 minute more. Add vinegar to the pan, turn off the heat, and toss to coat.

5. Divide the greens equally between two bowls. Spread them out to make a little well in the center, then drop an egg into each. Sprinkle each bowl with the bread crumbs and dash a bit more vinegar on top, if desired.

ZUCCHINI FRIES
WITH TZATZIKI

SERVES 4 AS AN APPETIZER

In an effort to reduce the time spent at the stovetop cooking eggplant destined for eggplant Parmesan, the brilliant team at *Cook's Illustrated* magazine devised an oven-frying technique. The method works equally well for zucchini, which emerges from the oven evenly golden and crisp, with creamy, tender centers. Breading the zucchini takes a bit of time but can be done in advance—you can store the breaded batons in the fridge for as long as a day. Make this dish at the height of the summer, when you are up to your eyeballs in zucchini and unloading any more on your neighbors is not an option. Served with a cool, minty tzatziki, your zucchini haul will never disappear so quickly.

1 large zucchini, about 10 inches long, cut into sticks (see Note)

¼ cup (32 g) all-purpose flour

1 egg

¾ cup Homemade Dried Bread Crumbs (page 178) or panko

¾ cup grated Parmigiano-Reggiano

Kosher salt and freshly cracked black pepper to taste

2 tablespoons neutral oil

Tzatziki, for serving (recipe follows)

NOTE: To prepare the zucchini, trim away each end and discard. Cut the zucchini in half crosswise to create two pieces 4 to 5 inches long. Cut each in half lengthwise through the center, then cut each half into ½-inch wedges. Trim away the thin, seedy center from each wedge and discard. You should be left with 4- to 5-inch sticks.

(recipe continues)

1. Place a rimmed sheet pan in the oven on the center rack and preheat it to 425°F.

2. In a large resealable plastic bag or large bowl, toss the zucchini with the flour. In a medium shallow dish with sides, beat the egg with 1 tablespoon water. In a separate medium shallow dish with sides, combine the bread crumbs and cheese, and season with salt and pepper to taste.

3. Working with three or four pieces at a time, remove the zucchini from the flour and dip each wedge into the eggs, allowing any excess to drip off, then coat evenly in the bread crumbs, pressing them to adhere. Lay the breaded zucchini on a small sheet pan or platter.

4. Remove the preheated sheet pan from the oven. Pour the oil over the sheet, tilting it to coat evenly. Lay the breaded sticks in a single layer on the hot sheet. Bake them until well browned and crisp on the first side, about 12 to 15 minutes. Flip and bake them until the second side is brown, another 7 to 10 minutes. Remove the pan from the oven. Serve the zucchini fries immediately with tzatziki.

Tzatziki

1 CUP

1 cup strained plain yogurt or Greek yogurt (see Notes)

2 tablespoons finely diced red onion

1 tablespoon finely chopped mint

1 garlic clove, minced (see Notes)

Kosher salt to taste

Fresh lemon juice

In a small bowl, stir together the yogurt, onion, mint, and garlic. Season with a pinch of salt and a squeeze of lemon juice. Taste and add more salt or lemon as needed. Cover the tzatziki and chill it until ready to use.

NOTES: To strain yogurt, line a sieve with cheesecloth and rest it over a medium bowl. Add 2 cups yogurt and let stand for several hours or overnight in the fridge, then discard the liquid that collects in the bowl.

If you find the bite of raw garlic unpleasant, blanch it in boiling water for 1 minute before mincing it.

WHITE BEAN GRATIN
WITH SAUSAGE

SERVES 3 TO 4 AS A SIDE DISH

When fully cooked beans are baked further in a shallow gratin dish, they soak up the liquid surrounding them, absorbing the flavors and becoming meltingly tender. In bean gratins, a small amount of a rich-flavored pork product goes a long way, by way of both its meaty presence dotting the beans and its seasonings permeating the broth. Here, fresh rosemary flavors the crispy bread-crumb topping, though sage or thyme would be fine substitutes, too. Remember to plan ahead: soaking the beans overnight will allow them to cook up in about an hour—but you can use canned if you prefer.

1 cup dried white beans, soaked overnight,
  or 2 (15-ounce) cans of Great Northern beans,
  drained and rinsed

1 small onion

2 lightly crushed garlic cloves

1 bay leaf

A few sprigs of fresh thyme

Pinch of crushed red pepper flakes

Kosher salt and freshly cracked black pepper

for the gratin

2 cups fresh bread crumbs (see Note, page 172)

2 garlic cloves, minced

½ teaspoon minced fresh rosemary

Zest of 1 lemon

Kosher salt

3 to 4 tablespoons extra-virgin olive oil

Freshly cracked black pepper

3 ounces smoked sausage, such as hot Italian or chorizo

1. If you're using dried beans, place them and their soaking liquid in a medium saucepan and cover with more water by at least 3 inches. Add the onion, garlic, bay leaf, thyme, and pepper flakes, and bring to a boil over high heat. Then reduce the heat to low and cook at the gentlest simmer your stovetop will allow until the beans are soft but not mushy, 45 minutes to 1 hour. Turn off the heat. Add ½ teaspoon of kosher salt and stir gently. Once the beans have cooled, at least 1 hour, taste and add more salt and pepper if necessary. Discard the bay leaf, onion, and thyme sprigs.

2. Make the gratin: Preheat the oven to 400°F.

3. Place the bread crumbs, garlic, rosemary, and lemon zest in a large bowl. Season with ½ teaspoon of kosher salt and 3 tablespoons of the oil, and toss to coat. The crumbs should be moist—add the additional tablespoon of oil if necessary. Taste and add more salt and pepper as needed.

4. Spoon the beans into a 9-inch baking pan. Cover the beans with their cooking liquid—they should be nearly submerged; if necessary, add enough water to almost cover them. If you are using canned beans, spread them into the baking dish, add 1 cup water, and season with ½ teaspoon kosher salt.

5. Halve the sausage lengthwise, then slice it into ¼-inch-thick half-moons. Scatter the pieces over the beans and push them down to submerge them in the liquid. Cover the whole dish with the bread crumbs.

6. Transfer the baking dish to the oven and bake until the bread crumbs are golden, 20 to 25 minutes. Remove the baking dish from the oven and let the gratin sit for 10 to 15 minutes before scooping it onto plates.

STUFFING TWO WAYS

Sometimes all you want is a no-frills stuffing: bread tossed with Bell's Seasoning, mixed with copious amounts of butter, onions, and celery; a stuffing that won't compete with the cranberry sauce, Aunt Phyllis's yams, and Alice Waters's potato gratin. But sometimes you want a stuffing, as Nigella Lawson says, "jumping around in a ra-ra skirt showing off its own." A stuffing studded with dried cranberries and chestnuts, laced with sweet onions (also sautéed in copious amounts of butter), strewn with kale that crisps up like chips as irresistible as the crusty cubes it surrounds. You can have both.

(recipe continues)

CLASSIC BREAD STUFFING

SERVES 8 TO 10

1½ pounds peasant bread (see page 22), crusts removed, torn into 1- to 2-inch pieces (about 12 cups)

½ cup extra-virgin olive oil

Kosher salt and freshly cracked black pepper

4 tablespoons (½ stick) unsalted butter

2 cups finely diced onions (1 to 2 onions)

1 cup finely diced celery

1 tablespoon Bell's Seasoning

1½ cups homemade Chicken Stock (page 183) or store-bought

1 egg

Softened unsalted butter, for greasing

1. Preheat the oven to 400°F. In a large bowl, toss the bread with ¼ cup oil; it will feel saturated. Season the bread with salt and pepper to taste. Spread it onto a sheet pan in a single layer, reserving the bowl. Transfer the pan to the oven and toast the bread for 15 to 17 minutes, or until golden. Set it aside to cool briefly.

2. Meanwhile, in a large sauté pan, melt the butter with the remaining ¼ cup oil over medium heat. Add the onions and celery, season with a pinch of salt, and cook for 5 to 10 minutes, stirring, until soft and beginning to color.

3. Return the toasted bread to the reserved bowl. When the onions and celery have finished cooking, scrape them into the bowl over the bread. Sprinkle with the Bell's. Add 1 cup chicken stock, ½ teaspoon salt, and ½ teaspoon pepper, and toss. Taste and adjust the seasoning, adding another ½ teaspoon salt and more pepper as needed. In a small bowl, whisk the remaining ½ cup chicken stock with the egg and add it to the bowl. Toss them to combine.

4. Grease a 9 × 13-inch baking pan with the softened butter and spread the mixture into it. Cover the pan with foil, transfer it to the center rack of the oven, and bake the stuffing for 30 minutes. Uncover the pan and bake the stuffing for 10 to 15 minutes more, until the bread is golden. Remove the stuffing and let it stand for 10 minutes before serving it.

STUFFING WITH KALE, CRANBERRIES, AND CHESTNUTS

SERVES 8 TO 10

1 pound peasant bread (see page 22), crusts
   removed, torn into 1- to 2-inch pieces (8 to 10 cups)

½ cup extra-virgin olive oil

Kosher salt

Freshly cracked black pepper

4 tablespoons (½ stick) unsalted butter

2 cups sliced onions (1 to 2 onions)

8 ounces kale, rough stems discarded, leaves sliced
   into ½-inch ribbons

⅓ cup dried cranberries

1 cup cooked chestnuts (optional) (see Note)

1½ cups homemade Chicken Stock (page 183)
   or store-bought

1 egg

Softened unsalted butter, for greasing

1. Preheat the oven to 400°F. In a large bowl, toss the bread with ¼ cup of the oil; the bread will feel saturated. Season with salt and pepper to taste. Spread onto a sheet pan in a single layer, reserving the bowl. Transfer to the oven and toast for 15 to 17 minutes, until golden. Set aside to cool briefly.

2. Meanwhile, in a large sauté pan, melt the butter with the remaining ¼ cup oil over medium heat. Add the onions, season with a pinch of salt, and cook, stirring, for 10 minutes, or until soft and beginning to color.

3. Place the kale in the reserved bowl and, when the onions have finished cooking, scrape them into the bowl over the kale. Add the dried cranberries, chestnuts, and bread, and toss. Add 1 cup of the chicken stock, ½ teaspoon salt, and ½ teaspoon pepper, and toss. Taste and adjust seasoning, adding another ½ teaspoon salt and pepper to taste as needed. In a small bowl, whisk the remaining ½ cup chicken stock with the egg and add to the bowl. Toss to combine.

4. Grease a 9 × 13-inch baking pan with the softened butter and spread the mixture into it. Cover the pan with foil, transfer it to the oven, and bake the stuffing for 30 minutes. Uncover the pan and bake the stuffing for 15 to 20 minutes more, until the bread is golden and the kale is beginning to crisp. Remove the pan from the oven and let the stuffing stand for 10 minutes before serving it.

NOTE: Cooked and peeled chestnuts can be found online or in specialty stores. Or you can cook them yourself: With a sharp knife, cut an X on both sides of each chestnut. Bring a small saucepan of water, filled halfway, to a boil over high heat. Add 8 ounces of chestnuts, reduce the heat to a simmer, and cook for 20 minutes, or until soft. Remove the pan from the heat. Using a slotted spoon, remove a few chestnuts at a time and run them under cold water. Peel and place the chestnuts in a small bowl. You may need to use a paring knife to remove the skin. You should have about 1 cup.

ORECCHIETTE
WITH BROWN BUTTER, BRUSSELS SPROUTS, AND CRUMBS

SERVES 3 TO 4

Peeling Brussels sprouts into individual leaves is a prodigious hassle, a task best undertaken with a good podcast streaming in the background or with the help of anyone lurking in your kitchen. But once you see that pile of mini green half shells ready to spoon with your pasta doppelgänger, the task will feel well worth the effort. And once the sprout peeling is complete, there's no other prep in this recipe—no nuts to toast, no onions to slice, no cheese to grate. Larger Brussels sprouts make for easier peeling, but if you're not up for it, you can buy or prepare shaved Brussels sprouts instead. Brown butter in combination with toasted bread crumbs gives this six-ingredient pasta a nutty, rich flavor.

6 tablespoons (¾ stick) unsalted butter

1 cup fresh bread crumbs (see Note, page 172)

¾ pound Brussels sprouts

1 tablespoon kosher salt, plus more as needed

½ pound orecchiette pasta

Freshly cracked black pepper to taste

1. Bring a large pot of water to a boil over high heat. Meanwhile, in a large sauté pan, melt 2 tablespoons of the butter over medium heat. Add the crumbs and toast until golden and crisp, 5 to 7 minutes, then transfer to a plate to cool. Wipe the skillet clean and melt the remaining 4 tablespoons of butter over medium heat. When the butter begins turning brown and smelling nutty, turn off the heat.

2. Meanwhile, prepare the Brussels sprouts. Halve the sprouts through the core, then use a paring knife to remove the triangular core in each half—this is the tedious part. When all the cores have been removed, pull the sprouts apart; some outer leaves will fall off easily, while others will need some tugging. When you reach the heart of the sprout where it is hard to remove the leaves, stop peeling and set the heart aside. After all of the sprouts are peeled, thinly slice the hearts.

3. When the water is boiling, add 1 tablespoon salt and the pasta. Check the cooking time on your package of pasta. Set a timer for 1 minute less than the time recommended for al dente, and when it dings, add the Brussels sprout leaves and hearts to the pot and cook for 1 minute more. Reserve ½ cup of the cooking liquid, then drain the pasta and sprouts.

4. Rewarm the brown butter over medium or medium-high heat. Add the pasta, sprouts, and some pepper. Taste and add more salt as needed. If the pasta is dry, add the reserved cooking liquid, 1 tablespoon at a time. Just before serving, add in the toasted bread crumbs and toss to combine.

SHEET-PAN MAC 'N' CHEESE

Who doesn't love the crunchy top layer of mac 'n' cheese? Baking this favorite dish in a sheet pan ensures a high ratio of crispy topping to creamy noodles. In this version, a layer of golden bread crumbs enshrouds blistered cubes of mozzarella, which stretch with every pull of the fork, clinging to the noodles trailing in its wake. This mac 'n' cheese can be cut into squares like sheet-pan pizza and needs nothing more than a simple green salad on the side.

12 ounces elbow macaroni

8 tablespoons (1 stick) unsalted butter

¼ cup unbleached all-purpose flour

2 cups whole milk

1 teaspoon kosher salt, plus more to taste

Freshly cracked black pepper to taste

3 cups lightly packed fresh bread crumbs
 (see Note, page 172)

½ cup finely chopped fresh parsley

2 cloves garlic, finely minced

1½ cups grated Parmigiano-Reggiano
 (about 4 ounces)

8 ounces fresh mozzarella, diced

1. Preheat the oven to 425°F. Bring a large pot of salted water to a boil over high heat. When the water is boiling, add the macaroni and cook for 5 minutes. Drain, but do not rinse. Set aside.

2. In the same large pot, melt 4 tablespoons of butter over medium-high heat. Add the flour, whisking constantly for about 1 minute. Add the milk and 2 cups water, whisking to pull up anything stuck to the bottom of the pan. Bring it to a boil, then reduce the heat to low. Add 1 teaspoon salt and pepper to taste. Simmer until the mixture begins to thicken—it should coat the back of a spoon—about 20 minutes. Remove the pot from the heat. Taste the béchamel and add more salt if necessary.

3. Meanwhile, melt the remaining 4 tablespoons of butter on the stovetop or in the microwave. Combine with the bread crumbs, parsley, and garlic in a medium bowl. Season with a pinch of salt and pepper to taste.

4. In a separate large bowl, toss the cooked macaroni with the grated Parmigiano-Reggiano. Add the béchamel and toss to coat.

5. Line the bottom of a rimmed sheet pan with parchment paper and spread the macaroni mixture on top. Scatter the mozzarella cubes around and top evenly with the bread-crumb mixture. Transfer the pan to the oven and bake the mac 'n' cheese for 25 to 30 minutes, until the top is golden and the macaroni is bubbling. Remove the pan from the oven and let the mac 'n' cheese sit for 10 minutes before serving.

ORZO GRATIN
WITH FETA, TOMATO, AND SHRIMP

SERVES 6

Shrimp with tomato and feta is a classic Greek dish often prepared as an appetizer and served in a two-handled *saganaki* pan. Here, shrimp and cubes of feta bake with orzo in an ouzo-spiked tomato sauce enlivened with parsley and tarragon. This is a great end-of-fall or winter dish when you're looking for a little brightness, though it can be made in the summer, too, using fresh tomatoes in place of the canned.

for the sauce

⅓ cup extra-virgin olive oil

2 cups finely chopped white or yellow onions (about 2 medium onions)

⅓ cup finely chopped fresh parsley

¼ cup ouzo or other anise-flavored liqueur

1 (28-ounce) can of peeled whole San Marzano tomatoes, crushed

Pinch of crushed red pepper flakes

Pinch of kosher salt

for the gratin

3 tablespoons unsalted butter

1 cup fresh bread crumbs (see Note, page 172)

1 cup dried orzo

½ teaspoon kosher salt, plus more as needed

Freshly cracked black pepper to taste

1 pound wild shrimp, 16 to 20 count, shelled, deveined, and cut into ¾-inch pieces

¼ cup finely chopped fresh parsley

¼ cup finely chopped fresh tarragon

¼ pound feta cheese, cut into ½-inch cubes

1. Make the sauce: In a medium saucepan, heat the olive oil over medium heat. When it begins to shimmer, add the onions and cook until they just begin to color, about 5 minutes. Stir in the parsley, then add the ouzo. Simmer for 2 to 3 minutes, until the alcohol smell dissipates. Add the tomatoes, the pepper flakes, and a generous pinch of salt. Cook at a steady simmer until the sauce begins to thicken, about 20 minutes. Remove the pan from the heat and set aside.

2. Make the gratin: Preheat the oven to 400°F. In a medium skillet, melt 2 tablespoons of the butter over medium heat. Add the bread crumbs and toast, stirring every so often, until golden, about 10 minutes. Remove and set aside.

3. Meanwhile, in a large ovenproof skillet, melt the remaining tablespoon butter over medium heat. Add the orzo, and toast, stirring constantly, until the orzo starts to brown. Stir in 2½ cups water, season with ½ teaspoon salt and pepper to taste, and bring to a boil. Cook at a low boil until the orzo is tender and the water has nearly evaporated, 8 to 10 minutes. Add the tomato sauce and stir to combine. Add the shrimp, parsley, and tarragon, and stir to distribute evenly. Scatter the feta on top, pressing down lightly to submerge the cubes halfway into the sauce. Sprinkle with the toasted crumbs.

4. Transfer the skillet to the oven and bake for 15 to 20 minutes, until bubbling and lightly golden. Remove the skillet from the oven and let the gratin sit for 5 minutes before serving.

LINGUINI
WITH WHITE WINE, CLAMS, AND CRUMBS

SERVES 4

Every time I make clams or mussels, I wonder why I don't make them more often—they demand little prep, take no time to cook, and taste exponentially more impressive than the effort they require. Here, a few pantry staples—butter, wine, a few sprigs of thyme—combine with crème fraîche and 2 pounds of littleneck clams, each a concentrated bouillon of the sea, preseasoned parcels chock-full of briny, full-flavored broth that releases upon steaming. Be sure to serve this on your largest, most dramatic platter, which will best allow the clams to trap the showering of crispy, herby crumbs.

1 tablespoons extra-virgin olive oil

⅓ cup fresh bread crumbs (see Note, page 172)

Pinch each of kosher salt and freshly cracked
  black pepper

½ pound linguine

6 tablespoons (¾ stick) unsalted butter

2 garlic cloves, minced

2 or 3 sprigs fresh thyme

4 tablespoons crème fraîche

½ cup white wine or prosecco

2 pounds small littleneck clams, rinsed and scrubbed

½ cup finely minced fresh parsley

1. Bring a large pot of water to a boil over high heat. In a medium sauté pan, heat the oil over medium heat. When it begins to shimmer, add the crumbs and toast them until golden and crisp, 5 to 7 minutes. Season with a pinch of salt and pepper. Transfer to a plate to cool.

2. When the water is boiling, add the pasta and cook until al dente, about 6 minutes. Drain and set aside.

3. Meanwhile, in a large pot, melt 4 tablespoons of the butter over low heat. Add the garlic and thyme sprigs and cook for 3 to 5 minutes, until the garlic is soft. Add the crème fraîche and wine, increase the heat to high, and bring to a simmer. Add the clams, cover, and cook for 3 to 5 minutes, until the clams open; discard any that do not. Add the pasta along with the remaining 2 tablespoons butter and parsley. Use tongs or two big spoons to toss the pasta in the cooking liquid to coat.

4. Transfer the clams, pasta, and broth to a large serving platter. Discard the thyme sprigs. Scatter the bread crumbs over the top and serve immediately.

BAKED PASTA
WITH MUSHROOMS, FONTINA, AND CRUMBS

SERVES 8 TO 10

A thin béchamel made with equal parts milk and water, a technique I learned from *Bon Appétit*, makes these baked shells taste surprisingly light, a feat for the genre of creamy casseroles. Moreover, the high ratio of béchamel to noodles precludes the need to parcook the pasta, which makes for super-easy assembly. A layer of parsley-speckled bread crumbs brightens this wintry dish.

¼ cup neutral oil

1¼ pounds cremini mushrooms, roughly chopped

2 tablespoons minced garlic

1 teaspoon minced fresh thyme

1 teaspoon kosher salt, plus more to taste

Freshly cracked black pepper

7 tablespoons unsalted butter

¼ cup all-purpose flour

3 cups whole milk

12 ounces shells or other pasta

1½ cups grated Parmigiano-Reggiano, (about 4 ounces)

2 cups fresh bread crumbs (see Note, page 172)

1 cup finely chopped fresh parsley

1 cup diced fontina cheese (about 8 ounces)

1. In a large sauté pan, heat 2 tablespoons oil over high heat. When it begins to shimmer, add half of the mushrooms and cook without stirring for 1 minute. Shake the pan and continue to cook until the mushrooms are browned, about 2 minutes more. Transfer to a bowl. Add the remaining 2 tablespoons oil to the same pan and when it begins to shimmer, repeat with the remaining mushrooms and transfer them to the same bowl. Season the mushrooms with garlic, thyme, and salt and pepper to taste. Toss to combine and set aside.

2. Preheat the oven to 400°F. In a large saucepan, melt 4 tablespoons butter over medium-high heat. Add the flour, whisking constantly for about 1 minute. Add the milk and 3 cups water, whisking to pull up anything stuck to the bottom of the pan. Bring to a boil, then reduce the heat to low. Add 1 teaspoon kosher salt and pepper to taste. Simmer until the mixture begins to thicken—it should lightly coat the back of a wooden spoon—15 to 20 minutes. Remove the pot from the heat. Taste the béchamel and add more salt if necessary.

3. In a 9 × 13-inch baking pan, toss the dry pasta with the grated Parmigiano-Reggiano. Add the mushrooms to the pan. Pour the béchamel over the top—it will feel like a lot of liquid, but it will all be absorbed during the baking. Gently stir to combine everything. Cover the pan with foil and carefully transfer it to the oven. Bake for 20 minutes.

4. Meanwhile, melt the remaining 3 tablespoons of butter on the stovetop or in the microwave. In a small bowl, combine it with the bread crumbs and parsley. Season with a pinch of kosher salt and pepper to taste.

5. Remove the pan from the oven and increase the temperature to 425°F. Remove the foil and gently stir the pasta. Scatter the cubes of fontina evenly and top with the bread-crumb mixture. Return the pan to the oven and bake the pasta, uncovered, for 20 to 25 minutes more, until the top is golden and the dish is bubbling. Remove the pan from the oven and let the pasta sit for 10 minutes before serving.

FRITTATA
WITH MUSTARD CROUTONS AND FONTINA

SERVES 2

Dressed in a mustard vinaigrette before toasting in the oven, shards of bread crisp into irresistible morsels. These chewy bites add texture to a frittata, where they soften and absorb the flavor of the eggs. Cubing the fontina, as opposed to grating it, allows it to suspend in the baked eggs, where it gently melts without totally disappearing. Any extra croutons can be tossed into a salad on the side, the perfect accompaniment for this simple dinner or lunch for two.

for the mustard croutons

2 tablespoons extra-virgin olive oil

1 tablespoon vinegar (white wine, red wine, cider, or white balsamic)

1 tablespoon Dijon mustard

¼ teaspoon kosher salt

Freshly cracked black pepper to taste

2 cups ¾-inch-cubed bread, such as peasant bread (see page 22), Three Seed Bread (page 28), Roasted Garlic Bread (page 49), Cheesy Cheddar and Parmigiano Bread (page 52), or Potato Bread (page 53)

for the frittata

1 tablespoon unsalted butter

¼ cup finely diced onion

Kosher salt and freshly cracked black pepper to taste

4 large eggs, beaten

½ cup ¼-inch-cubed fontina cheese

1. Make the mustard croutons: Preheat the oven to 400°F. In a large bowl, whisk together the oil, vinegar, mustard, salt, and pepper. Add the bread cubes and toss to coat. Spread onto a rimmed sheet pan in an even layer, transfer it to the oven, and bake for 10 to 12 minutes, until golden. Remove the pan from the oven and set it aside. Leave the oven on.

2. Make the frittata: In an 8-inch ovenproof nonstick skillet (see Note), melt the butter over high heat. Add the onion and immediately reduce the heat to medium. Season with salt and pepper. Sauté for 2 to 3 minutes, stirring occasionally, until the onions have softened slightly.

3. Add the beaten eggs to the skillet. Use a spatula to drag the edges of the eggs toward the center. Stir in this fashion for 1 to 2 minutes, until the eggs just begin to hold their shape. Add 1 cup of the mustard croutons and scatter the cheese on top.

4. Transfer the skillet to the oven and cook the frittata until just set, 2 to 5 minutes, keeping a close watch to prevent overcooking—the eggs will continue to cook out of the oven.

5. Remove the frittata from the oven, cut it into wedges, and serve.

NOTE: An ovenproof nonstick skillet is best for making this a hassle-free endeavor. This frittata bakes best on the small scale—an 8-inch pan allows for even and quick cooking.

SAVORY BREAD PUDDING
WITH BUTTERNUT SQUASH

SERVES 8 TO 10

Bread puddings, especially the savory sort, can be viewed as blank canvases, fit for cleaning out the fridge and using up whatever you have on hand. But for the right occasion, they can be thoughtfully fashioned, too. Here all of fall's favorite flavors unite: roasted squash and onions meet earthy herbs and a trio of cheeses. Bring this to an autumnal potluck or add it to your Thanksgiving spread, but consider giving your turkey fair warning: it may just be outshined.

4 cups diced onions (2 to 3 medium onions)

4 cups ¾-inch-cubed butternut squash

¼ cup extra-virgin olive oil

1½ teaspoons kosher salt

Freshly cracked black pepper

10 cups ¾-inch cubed day-old bread (14 ounces)

8 eggs

4 cups 2 percent or whole milk

1 tablespoon chopped fresh thyme

2 teaspoons chopped fresh rosemary

1 teaspoon chopped fresh sage

1½ cups grated Gruyère cheese

1 cup grated Parmigiano-Reggiano

¼ cup Gorgonzola or other blue cheese

Softened unsalted butter, for greasing

Freshly grated nutmeg (optional)

1. Preheat the oven to 325°F. In a rimmed sheet pan, toss the onions and squash with the oil, 1 teaspoon salt, and pepper to taste. Transfer to the oven and roast for 25 minutes, or until the squash is tender but not falling apart. Remove the pan from the oven.

2. Meanwhile, lay the bread in a single layer on a separate rimmed sheet pan. Transfer to the oven and bake for 15 minutes, or until slightly dry. Remove the pan from the oven and let the bread cool for 10 minutes. Leave the oven on.

3. In a large bowl, whisk together the eggs, milk, ½ teaspoon salt, a few grindings of pepper, thyme, rosemary, and sage until thoroughly combined. In a medium bowl, combine the cheeses. Add the roasted squash and onions, the bread cubes, and one-third of the cheeses to the bowl with the eggs and milk. Toss to combine.

4. Butter a 9 × 13-inch baking pan and pour the mixture into it—the pan will feel very full. Scatter the remaining cheese evenly on top. Grate a little nutmeg over it, if using.

5. Transfer the pan to the oven and bake for 45 minutes, or until the top of the pudding is golden and the surface feels firm to the touch. Remove the pan from the oven and let the pudding rest for 15 to 20 minutes before serving it.

CHICKPEA AND BEET BURGERS

SERVES 8

These burgers look to falafel for inspiration: soaked and puréed (but never cooked) chickpeas give body and texture to the patties, a method that lends itself to countless variations. Here, beets, herbs, and scallions combine with toasted pumpkin seeds to make the patties, though any number of vegetables, nuts, and seeds could be used in their place. A quick pan-frying creates a nice, golden crust, but you can bake them, too, at 350°F for 15 minutes, or until lightly golden with edges beginning to crisp. Serve them in Boston lettuce cups or Hamburger Buns (page 60) and drizzle with a simple cumin-yogurt sauce, which so nicely complements the beets' earthy sweetness. Be sure to plan ahead: the chickpeas must soak for at least 12 hours.

4 to 6 medium beets (12 to 14 ounces), washed (see Notes, page 212)

½ cup pumpkin seeds

½ cup dried chickpeas, soaked overnight and drained (see Notes, page 212)

2 to 3 scallions, ends trimmed, white and green parts roughly chopped

½ cup chopped fresh herbs, such as a mix of basil, cilantro, or parsley

1 teaspoon kosher salt, plus more as needed

Freshly cracked black pepper to taste

1 cup fresh bread crumbs (see Note, page 172)

1 egg, lightly beaten

¼ cup neutral oil, plus more as needed

Boston lettuce leaves or buns, for serving

Yogurt Sauce (recipe follows), for serving

1. Preheat the oven to 400°F. Place the beets on a large piece of aluminum foil and wrap them into a package, being sure the edges are sealed tightly. Place the package on a sheet pan, transfer it to the oven, and roast for 1 hour, or until tender when pierced with a knife. Remove the package from the oven, open carefully to allow the steam to escape, and set it aside to cool, about 20 minutes. Once the beets are cool enough to handle, rub off the skins and discard—you might want to wear gloves to do this. Roughly chop the beets; you should have about 2 cups.

2. Meanwhile, in a large skillet, toast the pumpkin seeds over medium heat, stirring, until they begin to brown and smell fragrant, 5 to 7 minutes. Transfer the seeds to a plate.

3. In the bowl of a food processor, place the drained chickpeas, roasted beets, toasted seeds, scallions, herbs, 1 teaspoon salt, and pepper. Pulse until blended, about 10 seconds. Scrape down the sides of the bowl and pulse again until combined; the mixture should be coarse. Transfer it to a large bowl. Taste and add more salt and pepper as needed. Add the bread crumbs and egg, and mix with your hands to combine.

4. Use a ⅓-cup measuring cup to portion the mixture into 8 patties. Pack and cup the portions between your hands as you shape each patty. If time permits, chill the patties for 30 minutes for easiest handling. (See Notes, page 212.)

(recipe continues)

5. In a large sauté pan, heat 2 tablespoons oil over medium-high heat. When it begins to shimmer, gently lower 4 patties into the oil. Season them with salt and pepper to taste. Reduce the heat to medium-low and cook for 2 to 3 minutes, until lightly golden on the bottom. Flip and cook the patties for 2 to 3 minutes more. Transfer them to a serving platter and repeat with remaining patties. Serve the burgers immediately in a lettuce cup or on the buns with yogurt sauce.

NOTES: The beets can be roasted ahead of time. Cool, peel, and store them in the refrigerator until you are ready to purée the chickpeas.

The formed patties can be stored in the fridge for up to 2 days. If storing the patties, layer them between pieces of parchment or wax paper and store in an airtight container.

Canned chickpeas cannot be used in place of soaked chickpeas—the texture will be too mushy.

Yogurt Sauce

MAKES ½ CUP

½ teaspoon whole cumin seeds or ground cumin

½ cup whole-milk plain yogurt

1 small garlic clove, minced

Pinch of kosher salt

Freshly cracked black pepper to taste

If using whole cumin seeds, crush them lightly with a mortar and pestle. In a small bowl, stir the yogurt with the cumin, garlic, salt, and pepper. Taste and adjust the seasoning as needed. Chill the yogurt sauce, covered, until ready to use.

TWICE-BAKED EGGPLANT PARMESAN

SERVES 4

Melanzane ripiene, stuffed eggplant, is the Italian version of twice-baked potatoes, its filling a blend of parcooked flesh and any number of seasonings, which typically reflect the offerings of the region where it is being made. In this version, onions, tomatoes, anchovies, and capers stew with the eggplant before binding with Parmigiano-Reggiano and fresh bread crumbs. After 45 minutes in the oven, the filling melds into the eggplant shells, creating a mass that is creamy in texture with a taste that evokes eggplant Parmesan. Although the *melanzane ripiene* can be served hot, the flavors are more pronounced when the eggplant cools to room temperature.

2 tablespoons extra-virgin olive oil, plus more for greasing

2 large eggplants (9 to 10 ounces each), halved lengthwise

Kosher salt

1 cup finely diced onions (about 1 medium onion)

2 garlic cloves, thinly sliced

1 cup diced tomatoes

2 anchovies, minced

1 tablespoon capers

1 to 2 tablespoons vinegar (red wine, white wine, or white balsamic)

1 cup fresh bread crumbs (see Note, page 172)

¾ cup grated Parmigiano-Reggiano, plus more for shaving

¼ cup finely chopped fresh basil

Freshly cracked black pepper to taste

1¼ cups tomato sauce, store-bought or Homemade Tomato Sauce (recipe follows)

1. Preheat the oven to 350°F. Lightly grease a 9 × 13-inch baking pan with oil. Season the halved eggplants generously with salt and place them cut-side down in the baking dish. Transfer the dish to the oven and roast the eggplant for 30 to 45 minutes, until the skins begin to wrinkle and the flesh is knife-tender. Remove the baking pan from the oven and, when cool enough to handle, use a spoon to scoop out the flesh of the eggplant into a small bowl, leaving a ¼-inch border all the way around. Set aside the hollowed-out eggplant; reserve the baking pan. Increase the oven temperature to 375°F.

2. Meanwhile, in a medium pan, heat 2 tablespoons oil over high heat. When it begins to shimmer, add the onion, garlic, and a pinch of salt. Cover, reduce the heat to low, and cook for 15 minutes, or until the onions have softened.

3. Uncover the pot and add the diced tomato, anchovies, and eggplant flesh. Cover the pot again and cook for 15 minutes more, or until the tomato has completely softened. Uncover the pot once more, increase the heat to medium, and cook for 5 minutes, or until the juices reduce slightly. Add the capers and 1 tablespoon of vinegar, stir to combine, and cook for 1 minute more. Taste and add the remaining tablespoon of vinegar for more bite, if desired.

(recipe continues)

4. In a large bowl, combine the bread crumbs and cheese. Add the eggplant mixture and basil and stir to combine. Season with more salt and pepper to taste.

5. Spread 1 cup of tomato sauce across the bottom of the reserved baking dish, and arrange the hollowed eggplant on top. Divide the eggplant mixture evenly among the eggplant shells and spoon 1 tablespoon of tomato sauce over each. Transfer the dish to the oven and bake for 45 minutes, or until the filling has melded into the shell and the sauce is caramelizing at the edges.

6. Remove the eggplant from the oven. Shave more cheese over the top. Let it stand at least 10 minutes before serving it.

Homemade Tomato Sauce

MAKES 1½ CUPS

1 tablespoon extra-virgin olive oil

½ cup diced onion

2 garlic cloves, minced

Kosher salt

Pinch of crushed red pepper flakes

2 cups diced tomatoes

¼ cup finely chopped fresh basil

1. In a medium pan, heat the oil over high heat. When it begins to shimmer, add the onion, immediately turn the heat to low, cover, and sweat until soft, about 15 minutes.

2. Add the garlic, a pinch of salt, pepper flakes, and the tomatoes, stir, cover the pan, and simmer over low heat for 10 minutes or until the tomatoes begin to break down. Uncover the pan, increase the heat to medium-low, and cook for 10 minutes more, or until the juices have evaporated and the sauce has thickened.

3. Stir in the basil. Taste and adjust the seasoning with more salt or pepper flakes as needed. Remove the pan from the heat and set aside to cool.

ANTONIETTA'S PANCOTTO

SERVES 4 TO 6

Pancotto falls into the vast family of bread-thickened soups created by resourceful cooks in lean times. In essence, it is "cooked bread" and can be made with little more than water, garlic, and greens, though throughout Italy it is made in countless ways. I learned this version from a friend's mother, Antonietta Fazzone, who is like the *nonna* you've only read about—she makes her own wine and prosciutto, gardens, preserves everything, and measures nothing when she cooks.

When she made *pancotto* for me, she began by cutting garlic directly into a pot of oil. Then she added homegrown broccoli rabe and water, seasoned to taste, and fed me lemon-glazed anisette cookies. While it simmered, she added water here and there as needed, until the broth tasted right. Just before serving, she added torn hardened bread, which swelled and broke down as she stirred constantly. In just over a minute, the bread and greens melded into a unified mass, which pulled from the sides of the pot, every drop of broth absorbed by the undulating unit of greens and bread.

Pancotto is considered peasant food, but it is one of the most comforting, delicious meals imaginable, and somehow, without butter or stock, it tastes rich. Antonietta notes that lots of olive oil is the key.

1 pound peasant bread (see page 22), cut into ½-inch slices

1 to 1¼ pounds greens, such as broccoli rabe (stems removed) or escarole (see Notes, page 182), cut into 1-inch pieces

¼ cup extra-virgin olive oil, plus more for drizzling

6 garlic cloves, minced

Crushed red pepper flakes to taste (optional)

Kosher salt and freshly cracked black pepper to taste

1. Preheat the oven to 350°F. Bring a large pot of water to a boil over high heat. Lay out the slices of bread on a sheet pan. Transfer to the oven and toast for 20 minutes, or until lightly brown and crisp to the touch. Remove the pan from the oven and set it aside.

2. When the water comes to a boil, add the greens and cook for 1 minute, then drain and run them under cold water. Set them aside to drain in a colander.

3. In a medium pan, heat the oil over low heat. When it begins to shimmer, add the garlic and cook for 3 to 4 minutes, until just beginning to color. Add the pepper flakes, if using, and greens and stir to coat. Add 4 cups water, increase the heat to high, and bring to a simmer. Season generously with salt and pepper. Reduce the heat to low, cover the pan, and gently simmer for 45 minutes.

4. Meanwhile, break the toasted bread into 1-inch pieces and place in a large bowl.

5. After the 45 minutes, uncover the pot, increase the heat to medium, and add the bread—it will feel like a lot—and stir constantly to incorporate. In 1 to 2 minutes, all the broth should be absorbed, and the bread and greens should meld into one unified mass.

6. Drizzle the mixture with olive oil and stir to incorporate. Remove the pan from the heat, and scoop the *pancotto* into bowls. Season with more salt and pepper to taste and drizzle with more olive oil, if desired.

CRISPY TARRAGON CUTLETS

SERVES 2 GENEROUSLY

This preparation of chicken cutlets forgoes the traditional three-station (flour, egg, crumb) breading procedure for a simple mixture of mayonnaise, mustard, and fresh tarragon. While these cutlets do not need to be pounded as thinly as when making schnitzel or scaloppine, it is important that the breasts be ½ inch thick or less, which will allow them to cook evenly and completely on the stovetop. The simplified breading process and quick cooking time make this an easy weeknight dinner and a delicious one to boot—adults and children alike will love it.

2 boneless, skinless chicken breast halves
  (4 to 5 ounces each)

Kosher salt and freshly cracked black pepper
  to taste

3 tablespoons mayonnaise

1 tablespoon Dijon mustard

¼ cup finely chopped fresh tarragon

1 cup Homemade Dried Bread Crumbs (page 178)
  or panko

¼ cup neutral oil, plus more as needed

1. Wrap the chicken breasts in parchment paper or plastic wrap to protect them and pound the meat to a thickness of ½ inch. Halve each pounded breast to create four roughly equal pieces. Season the meat all over lightly with salt and pepper.

2. In a large bowl, whisk together the mayonnaise, mustard, and tarragon. Add the breasts and turn to coat them evenly.

3. Pour the crumbs into a large shallow dish. Working with one or two pieces of chicken at a time, coat the breasts in crumbs, patting them to adhere. Transfer the chicken to a clean plate.

4. In a large skillet, heat the oil over medium-high heat. When it begins to shimmer, add the chicken, as many pieces as can fit without crowding, and immediately reduce the heat to medium-low. Cook the chicken breasts for 2 to 3 minutes per side, until evenly golden. Repeat with any remaining chicken, adding more oil as necessary. Serve immediately.

FISH STICKS
WITH TARTAR SAUCE

SERVES 3 TO 4

A general rule of thumb when calculating how much fish to buy for dinner is half a pound per person. But when fish is cut into strips, then breaded and fried, that rule holds less weight—the simple addition of bread crumbs allows a one-pound piece of fish to feed three or four people. Here, a homemade mayonnaise plays double duty, first as the glue that adheres the crumbs to the fish, second as the dipping sauce. Mixed with a hard-boiled egg, herbs, shallots, capers, and cornichons, it becomes at once a creamy and textured tartar sauce.

2 eggs

2 teaspoons Dijon mustard

1 tablespoon vinegar (white balsamic or white wine), or lemon juice, plus more as needed

Kosher salt and freshly cracked black pepper

1 cup neutral oil, plus more for frying

¼ cup finely chopped chives

2 tablespoons finely chopped shallots

1 tablespoon capers, rinsed

1 pound wild sole or flounder, skinned and cut into 4 × 1-inch strips

3 to 4 finely chopped cornichons

Juice of 1 lemon

1 cup Homemade Dried Bread Crumbs (page 178) or panko

Lemon wedges, for serving

1. In a small saucepan, place 1 egg and add enough cold water to cover. Bring to a boil over high heat, then immediately turn off the heat. Let the egg sit in the pan for 15 minutes. Drain and transfer to a bowl of cold water and let sit for at least 2 minutes. When cool enough to handle, peel the egg and chop it finely.

2. Meanwhile, in the bowl of a food processor, place the remaining egg, the mustard, vinegar, a pinch of salt, and pepper to taste and pulse to combine. With the motor running, slowly stream in 1 cup of the oil. Taste and adjust the seasoning as needed. Transfer the mayonnaise to a small bowl.

3. Fold the chives, shallots, and capers into the mayonnaise. Transfer ¼ cup of the mixture to a large bowl and add the sole. Gently turn the strips to coat, then set aside. Fold the hard-boiled egg and cornichons into the remaining mayonnaise in the small bowl to make the tartar sauce. Taste and add a squeeze of lemon or more vinegar as needed. Chill the tartar sauce, covered, until ready to serve.

4. Place the crumbs in a shallow dish. Add the sole, pressing the crumbs to adhere.

5. Heat 2 tablespoons of oil in a large sauté pan over high heat. When it shimmers, add as many strips of fish as will fit without crowding. Immediately reduce the heat to medium. Cook until golden on the bottom, about 2 minutes. Flip and cook for 1 to 2 minutes more. Repeat with the remaining fish, adding more oil to the pan as needed.

6. Serve immediately with the tartar sauce and lemon wedges.

MUSTARD-ROASTED CHICKEN
WITH LEMON-THYME BREAD CRUMBS

SERVES 4 TO 6

Encrusted in lemon-and-thyme bread crumbs, mustard-slicked chicken drumsticks emerge from the oven golden and crispy, a good alternative to fried chicken without all the fuss. Prep time here is minimal and the payoff is big: tender meat falling off the bone and herby bread crumbs spilling all around.

3 tablespoons Dijon mustard

6 tablespoons extra-virgin olive oil

8 bone-in chicken drumsticks (about 1½ pounds), skin removed

Kosher salt and freshly cracked black pepper

2 garlic cloves

Zest of 1 lemon

1 teaspoon fresh thyme leaves

2 cups fresh bread crumbs (see Note, page 172)

1. Place a rack in the middle of the oven and preheat it to 400°F. In a large bowl, whisk together the mustard and 3 tablespoons of the oil. Add the chicken and toss to coat. Season lightly with salt and pepper to taste.

2. Place the garlic, zest, thyme, ½ teaspoon salt, and a few cracks of pepper in a food processor and purée until the garlic is finely minced. Add the bread crumbs and the remaining 3 tablespoons oil, and pulse a few more times just to moisten the bread crumbs. Pour the mixture into a wide, shallow bowl.

3. Line a sheet pan with parchment paper. Roll each piece of chicken into the crumb mixture, pressing them gently to adhere. Place the chicken on the sheet pan, spacing the pieces in a single layer. Transfer the pan to the oven and bake the chicken for 45 to 55 minutes, until the crumbs are browned and the meat is starting to pull away from the bone. Remove the pan from the oven and let the chicken rest for 5 to 10 minutes before serving it.

BROILED STRIPED BASS
WITH CAPERS AND CRUMBS

SERVES 2

Pan-frying fillets of fish requires a deft hand. Instead, this method employs the broiler and an ovenproof skillet, which makes flipping unnecessary while still ensuring the fish cooks through completely. Mustard crumbs crisp over a thin layer of caper-studded mayonnaise, which protect the fish's delicate flesh, ensuring it will be moist and flaky. Serve with a squeeze of fresh lemon and roasted potatoes alongside.

2 tablespoons extra-virgin olive oil

2 fillets skin-on striped bass (6 ounces each), ½-inch thick (see Note)

Kosher salt and freshly cracked black pepper

1 tablespoon mayonnaise

2 teaspoons Dijon mustard

1 teaspoon capers

½ cup fresh bread crumbs (see Note, page 172)

Lemon wedges, for serving

1. Preheat the broiler to high with a rack set 4 inches from the heat. Place 1 tablespoon of the oil in a 9-inch ovenproof skillet. Lay the fish fillets on the oil, skin-side down, and season lightly with salt and pepper.

2. In a small bowl, whisk together the mayonnaise, 1 teaspoon of the mustard, and the capers. In a separate small bowl, combine the bread crumbs with the remaining 1 tablespoon oil and 1 teaspoon mustard. Use your fingers to mix, ensuring the crumbs are saturated. Spread the mayonnaise mixture evenly over the fish fillets. Spread the bread crumb mixture on top, pressing it to adhere. Season with pepper.

3. Transfer the skillet to the oven and broil the fish until the bread crumbs are golden brown, about 5 minutes. Remove the pan from the oven and place it on a burner over high heat for 1 to 2 minutes, until the fish is cooked through. Transfer the fish to plates and serve it with lemon wedges.

NOTE: The method here works for any thin fillets of fish no thicker than ½ inch. If you would like to use a thicker piece, simply roast at 500°F for about 8 minutes per inch. Finished fish should flake easily when tested with a fork.

RACK OF LAMB
WITH BREAD-CRUMB CHIMICHURRI

SERVES 2

When *pangrattato* (see page 166) is taken one step further—when the toasty crumbs are bathed in oil, vinegar or lemon, and a showering of herbs—it becomes a sauce, a bright, textured chimichurri fit for spooning over grilled skirt steak, pan-seared duck breast, or, as here, rack of lamb. Adjust the herbs depending on what you are serving: tarragon and parsley pair especially well with chicken, chives with fish, cilantro with beef, thyme and orange zest with duck, and mint with lamb. A little heat is nice, too—a pinch of crushed red pepper flakes or a minced jalapeño. And don't limit the use of this sauce to meat: toss it with pasta, drizzle it over fried or poached eggs, or swirl it into Roasted Tomato and Bread Soup (page 185).

1 rack of lamb, 1½ to 1¾ pounds, room temperature (see Note)

Kosher salt and freshly cracked black pepper

1 teaspoon dried oregano

2 tablespoons Dijon mustard

2 to 3 tablespoons extra-virgin olive oil

Bread-Crumb Chimichurri (recipe follows)

Lemon wedges, for serving

NOTE: Racks of lamb vary in thickness and weight. If you have a very thin rack, weighing up to 1¼ pounds, reduce the cooking time by 5 minutes.

1. Preheat the oven to 500°F. If your rack of lamb has not been trimmed, shave off the fat, leaving a thin layer, ⅛ to ¼ inch thick; you want just enough fat to protect the meat. Season the lamb all over with salt and pepper. Sprinkle with oregano.

2. In a small bowl with a small whisk or fork, whip the mustard and oil together until emulsified like mayonnaise. Spread the mixture all over the top, sides, and underside of the rack.

3. Cover a sheet pan with aluminum foil and add the rack, fat-side up, to the pan. Transfer to the oven and roast for 10 minutes, then reduce the temperature to 400°F and roast for about 10 minutes more, or until golden and until a thermometer registers 135°F for medium rare.

4. Remove the pan from the oven, transfer the lamb to a serving platter or cutting board, and let it rest 10 to 15 minutes. Spoon the bread-crumb chimichurri all over. Slice the lamb into the ribs to separate. Serve the lamb with wedges of lemon and more chimichurri on the side.

Bread-Crumb Chimichurri

MAKES 1 CUP

⅓ cup plus 1 tablespoon extra-virgin olive oil

½ cup fresh bread crumbs (see Note, page 172)

¼ cup coarsely chopped fresh mint

¼ cup coarsely chopped fresh parsley

¼ cup freshly squeezed lemon juice (1 to 2 lemons)

1 shallot, finely minced (about 2 tablespoons)

¼ to ½ teaspoon crushed red pepper flakes

¼ teaspoon fine sea salt

1. In a medium skillet, heat 1 tablespoon of oil over medium heat. When it begins to shimmer, add the bread crumbs and stir until toasted, 5 to 10 minutes, watching carefully to prevent burning. Transfer the crumbs to a plate and set it aside.

2. Combine the remaining ⅓ cup oil with the mint, parsley, lemon juice, shallot, ¼ teaspoon pepper flakes, and salt. Set it aside. Combine with the bread crumbs just before using it. Taste. Adjust seasoning as desired.

MEATBALLS
THREE WAYS

We know that for centuries Italian grandmothers have been reviving petrified heels of bread with milk, mixing in whatever leftover meat they have on hand, ingeniously transforming scraps into comforting *polpettes*—meatballs. But we also know that the key to making featherlight meatballs and meat loaves is to mix the ground meat with a *panade*—a starch (bread, crackers, oatmeal) soaked in liquid (wine, milk, buttermilk, stock, water).

So which is it? Were *nonnas* making do with what they had? Or all along, was thrift the secret to their extra-tender *polpettes*? Maybe it's both, and we certainly can conclude that day-old bread is a miracle worker, not only extending food, but also working gastronomically in our favor.

(recipe continues)

BROILED LAMB MEATBALLS

MAKES 18 TO 20 (1-INCH) MEATBALLS

2 slices peasant bread (see page 22), ½ inch thick, crusts removed (about 2 ounces)

2 tablespoons wine (red, white, or rosé)

1 pound ground lamb

1 teaspoon kosher salt, plus more as needed

Freshly cracked black pepper to taste

½ cup minced onion

1 egg, lightly beaten

1 teaspoon dried oregano, plus more for sprinkling

¼ cup finely chopped fresh mint

¼ cup finely chopped fresh parsley

1 tablespoon extra-virgin olive oil, plus more for the pans

Lemon wedges or vinegar, for serving

1. Preheat the oven to 300°F. Lay the bread on a sheet pan in a single layer, transfer to the oven, and toast for 10 minutes, or just until it is slightly dry. Remove the pan from the oven and set it aside to cool for 5 minutes. Crumble the bread into a small bowl and pour the wine over it. Let it stand for 10 minutes, or until the bread absorbs the liquid.

2. Meanwhile, in a large bowl, spread out the lamb and season with salt and pepper. Add the onion, egg, oregano, mint, parsley, and 1 tablespoon olive oil. Crumble the wine-soaked bread over the top. Mix it well with your hands until thoroughly combined. Refrigerate it, covered, for at least 1 hour.

3. Preheat the broiler to high, with a rack 4 inches from the heat source. Rub a little oil over a sheet pan. Using a tablespoon measure, shape the lamb mixture into

ping-pong-size balls; the mixture will be rounding out of the measure. Place the meatballs on the prepared pan. Season lightly with salt, pepper, and a pinch more of oregano. Transfer the pan to the oven and broil the meatballs for 3 to 4 minutes, until lightly browned. Turn them over and broil for 3 to 4 more minutes. Remove the meatballs from the oven and spoon any pan juices over them. Serve the meatballs with lemon wedges or sprinkle them with vinegar to taste.

ROASTED BEEF MEATBALLS

MAKES 12 (2-INCH) MEATBALLS

2 slices peasant bread (see page 22), ½ inch thick, crusts removed (about 2 ounces)

2 tablespoons 2 percent or whole milk

1 pound 80/20 ground beef

1 teaspoon kosher salt, plus more as needed

Freshly cracked black pepper to taste

½ cup finely minced red onion

1 egg, lightly beaten

1 tablespoon extra-virgin olive oil, plus more for the pan (optional) and for brushing

¼ cup finely chopped fresh parsley

½ teaspoon dried oregano

½ teaspoon fennel seed

Pinch of crushed red pepper flakes

1. Preheat the oven to 300°F. Lay the bread in a single layer on a sheet pan, transfer the pan to the oven, and toast the bread for about 10 minutes, just until it is slightly dry. Remove the pan from the oven and set aside to cool for 5 minutes. Leave the oven on and increase the temperature to 450°F.

2. Crumble the bread into a small bowl and pour the milk over it. Let stand for 10 minutes, or until the bread absorbs the liquid.

3. Meanwhile, in a large bowl, spread out the beef. Season with 1 teaspoon salt and black pepper to taste. Add the onion, egg, 1 tablespoon olive oil, parsley, oregano, fennel seed, and pepper flakes. Scatter the milk-soaked bread over the top. Mix well with your hands until thoroughly combined.

4. Line a sheet pan with parchment paper or rub lightly with oil. Using a ¼-cup measure, form the beef mixture into ten to twelve 2-inch balls and place on the prepared pan; preferably, if time permits, refrigerate, covered, for 1 hour. Season lightly all over with salt and pepper as needed. Brush a little oil on top. Transfer the pan to the oven and roast the meatballs for 10 to 12 minutes, until lightly browned on top and firm to the touch. Remove the meatballs from the oven and let them rest for 5 minutes before serving them.

PAN-FRIED TURKEY MEATBALLS

MAKES 18 TO 20 (1-INCH) MEATBALLS

2 slices peasant bread (see page 22), ½ inch thick, crusts removed (about 2 ounces)

6 tablespoons buttermilk

1 pound ground turkey

¾ teaspoon kosher salt, plus more as needed

Freshly cracked black pepper to taste

1 egg, lightly beaten

1 teaspoon Worcestershire sauce

½ cup finely diced red onion

¼ cup finely chopped scallions, white and green parts

2 tablespoons finely chopped fresh parsley

4 tablespoons neutral oil, for frying

1. Preheat the oven to 300°F. Lay the bread in a single layer on a sheet pan, transfer the pan to the oven, and toast the bread for 10 minutes, or just until it is slightly dry. Remove the pan from the oven and set it aside to cool for 5 minutes. Crumble the bread into a small bowl and pour the buttermilk over it. Let it stand for about 10 minutes, or until the bread absorbs the liquid.

2. Meanwhile, in a large bowl, spread out the turkey. Season with ¾ teaspoon salt and pepper. Add the egg, Worcestershire, onion, scallions, and parsley. Scatter the buttermilk-soaked bread on top. Mix well with your hands until thoroughly combined.

3. Using a tablespoon measure, shape the meatballs into ping-pong-size balls; the mixture will be rounding out of the measure. Transfer to a small platter.

4. In a large frying pan, heat 2 tablespoons of the oil over high heat. When it begins to shimmer, immediately reduce the heat to low. Add as many meatballs to the pan as will fit without crowding. Season with salt and pepper and cook for 2 to 3 minutes, until golden. Use a fork or spoon to flip the meatballs over and brown the other side for another 2 minutes. Transfer the meatballs to a serving platter. Repeat with the remaining meatballs, adding the remaining 2 tablespoons oil to the pan as needed. Let the meatballs rest for 5 minutes before serving them.

VIRGIE'S MEAT LOAF

SERVES 8 TO 10

Baked in a loaf pan or freeform; glazed or naked; bound by grains, saltines, or gelatin—varied are the methods for making meat loaf. But in essence, meat loaf is a giant meatball: a dish born of economy, a way to feed many mouths with inexpensive meat. Here the meat is kept moist by a buttermilk *panade* and a mix of ketchup, mustard, and Worcestershire. This version is old-fashioned to the core—your mama's meat loaf, or even your mama's mama's meat loaf. And if she's anything like mine, she would be tickled knowing you were still making it.

2 cups fresh bread crumbs (see Note, page 172)

½ cup buttermilk

2 tablespoons extra-virgin olive oil

2 cups finely chopped onions (1 to 2 medium onions)

½ cup ketchup

1 tablespoon Dijon mustard

1 tablespoon Worcestershire sauce

A few dashes of Tabasco (optional)

2 eggs

1 pound 80/20 ground chuck

1 pound ground pork

1½ teaspoons kosher salt, plus more as needed

1 teaspoon freshly cracked green or black pepper, plus more as needed

1 teaspoon dried oregano

1 teaspoon finely chopped fresh thyme

½ teaspoon freshly ground juniper berries

½ cup finely chopped fresh parsley

1 tablespoon unsalted butter, cut into small pieces

1. Preheat the oven to 375°F. Place the bread crumbs in a medium bowl and pour the buttermilk over them. Set aside to soak until the crumbs have absorbed nearly all of the buttermilk, about 10 minutes.

2. Meanwhile, in a large skillet, heat the oil over high heat. When it begins to shimmer, add the onion, reduce the heat to medium, and sauté until soft and just beginning to color, about 5 minutes.

3. Line a rimmed sheet pan with aluminum foil or parchment paper. In a medium bowl, whisk together the ketchup, mustard, Worcestershire, Tabasco (if using), and eggs.

4. In a large bowl, spread out the ground meat. Season all over with 1½ teaspoons salt, 1 teaspoon pepper, oregano, thyme, and ground juniper berries. Scatter the onions, ketchup mixture, buttermilk-soaked bread crumbs, and parsley on top. Mix with your hands to incorporate and evenly distribute all the ingredients.

5. Transfer the mixture to the prepared sheet pan and shape it into a uniform loaf about 3 to 4 inches wide. Season all over with salt and pepper. Dot the surface with the butter.

6. Transfer the meat loaf to the center rack of the oven and bake for 40 to 45 minutes, until the meat has browned and the top feels firm to the touch. Remove the pan from the oven and let it sit for 10 minutes before serving.

BLUEBERRY BROWN BETTY

SERVES 8 TO 10

The brown Betty falls into the genre of warm, bubbling, crumb-topped fruit desserts, and perhaps is the simplest and most economical of all. Whereas cobblers and crisps call for biscuits or nut-and-oat toppings, Betties call for bread crumbs, flavored simply with butter and sugar. These sweetened crumbs play double duty, too, acting not only as the topping but also as the thickening agent for the juicy, stewing fruit, rendering flour or cornstarch unnecessary.

Softened unsalted butter, for greasing

6 cups blueberries (see Note)

½ cup plus 3 tablespoons sugar

Juice of ½ a lemon

Pinch of kosher salt

4 lightly filled cups fresh bread crumbs (see Note, page 172)

8 tablespoons (1 stick) unsalted butter, melted

Vanilla ice cream or heavy cream, for serving

1. Preheat the oven to 350°F. Grease an 8- or 9-inch ovenproof skillet or baking pan. In a large bowl, toss the blueberries with ½ cup sugar, lemon juice, and salt. In a separate large bowl, mix the crumbs with the melted butter and 3 tablespoons sugar.

2. Layer half the blueberries into the prepared skillet. Top with one-third of the crumb mixture. Layer the remaining blueberries over the top. Finish with the remaining crumbs.

3. Transfer the skillet to the oven and bake for 45 to 50 minutes, until the top is golden and the edges are bubbling. Remove the skillet from the oven and let it cool for 10 minutes before serving the brown Betty with ice cream or heavy cream.

NOTE: This recipe can be made with other fruits, too. For an autumnal variation, use 6 to 8 apples, peeled and thinly sliced, and add ½ teaspoon cinnamon with the sugar.

BRIOCHE BREAD PUDDING

SERVES 8 TO 10

This recipe adheres to the same egg-to-liquid ratio applied to every custard-based recipe in this book (see page 142), but here the whites have been removed. Egg whites, whose proteins provide structure, enable custard-based dishes to hold their shape when cut. When they are removed from the equation, the texture of the custard becomes as silky smooth as crème brûlée, unable to hold its shape on the plate, buckling around saturated cubes of brioche. Trust me—you wouldn't want it any other way.

10 cups ¾-inch-cubed bread (14 ounces), such as Light Brioche (page 92)

8 egg yolks

¾ cup plus 2 tablespoons sugar

2 cups heavy cream

2 cups 2 percent or whole milk

2 teaspoons vanilla extract

1 teaspoon kosher salt

Softened unsalted butter, for greasing

2 tablespoons (¼ stick) unsalted butter, melted

1. Preheat the oven to 325°F. Lay the bread in a single layer on a rimmed sheet pan. Transfer the pan to the oven and bake the bread for 15 minutes. Remove the pan from the oven and let the bread cool for 15 minutes.

2. In a large bowl, whisk together the yolks, ¾ cup sugar, the cream, milk, vanilla, and salt. Grease a 9 × 13-inch baking pan, and spread the cooled bread in the pan. Pour the custard over it and let it stand for 30 minutes.

3. Brush the melted butter on top, then sprinkle with 2 tablespoons sugar. Transfer the pan to the oven and bake for about 45 minutes, or until the custard is just set. Remove the pan from the oven and let the bread pudding cool for 20 minutes before serving it.

HOMEMADE CHOCOLATE BARK
WITH CARAMELIZED CRUMBS AND SEA SALT

MAKES 12 OUNCES BARK

Cloaked in dark and white chocolate, bedazzled with sea salt, here bread crumbs get all dolled up for the holidays. This homemade chocolate bark evokes a Krackel bar or Nestle's Crunch, a nut-free festive treat to gift to friends—or to snack on all winter long.

6 ounces white chocolate, broken into pieces

6 ounces dark chocolate, 70% cacao, such as Scharffen Berger or Valrhona, broken into pieces

2 tablespoons sugar

Pinch of kosher salt

¼ cup Homemade Dried Bread Crumbs (page 178) or panko

1 tablespoon unsalted butter

Sea salt, for sprinkling

1. Cut a piece of parchment paper into a large rectangle and place it on a rimmed sheet pan.

2. In a small bowl set over gently simmering water, melt the white chocolate. (Alternatively, place it in a small, microwave-safe bowl and warm it at 30-second intervals until the chocolate is melted.) In a separate small bowl set over gently simmering water, melt the dark chocolate. (Alternatively, place it in a separate, small microwave-safe bowl and warm it at 30-second intervals until melted.) Keep melted chocolate warm.

3. Meanwhile, in a small pot over medium-high heat, combine the sugar, salt, and 1 tablespoon water. Bring to a boil, then reduce the heat to medium. Cook the sugar mixture just until it starts to color— it should be light amber. Remove the pot from the heat, add the crumbs and butter, and stir to coat the crumbs and melt the butter. If necessary, set the pan over low heat and stir until the butter melts. The crumbs should be lightly golden and the texture of cookie crumbs. Transfer the crumbs to a large plate to cool, about 5 minutes. Set aside 1 tablespoon of the crumbs for sprinkling over the finished bark.

4. Pour the melted white chocolate into the parchment-lined sheet pan. Using an offset spatula, spread the chocolate to the edges of the parchment. Sprinkle all but the reserved 1 tablespoon of crumbs evenly over the top. Chill the chocolate in the fridge, covered, until set, about 15 minutes.

5. Remove the pan from the fridge and spread the melted dark chocolate over the white chocolate layer. Transfer the pan back to the fridge to chill for 10 minutes.

6. Remove the pan from the fridge, sprinkle it lightly with sea salt and the reserved bread crumbs, and return it to the fridge to cool completely, at least 1 hour. Remove the pan from the fridge, break the chocolate into shards, transfer the bark to an airtight container, and store it in the fridge.

FRIED CUSTARD CREAM

MAKES 24 BALLS

Fried custard cream is exactly as it sounds: deep-fried custard, like the inside of a Boston cream doughnut, in a shell of crispy, golden crumbs. In Italy, it is served for dessert or as part of a savory *fritto misto*, a mix of fried vegetables, fish, and meat often served as the first course. This custard is similar to crème pâtissière, but with more flour, which makes it thicker, allowing it to be scooped and breaded. Be sure to plan ahead: the custard must be chilled for at least an hour before being scooped, and the shaped balls must chill again before being fried. Once assembled, however, these balls can be frozen for months. Fry these after dinner, dust with confectioners' sugar, and eat immediately—in one bite, if you can, as the lemony custard spills out upon contact.

2 eggs

¼ cup plus 2 tablespoons sugar

Zest of 1 lemon

¼ teaspoon kosher salt

¼ cup plus 2 tablespoons unbleached all-purpose flour

1 cup whole milk

¾ cups Homemade Dried Bread Crumbs (page 178) or panko

2 cups oil (canola, vegetable, or peanut oil), for frying

Confectioners' sugar, for serving

1. Fill a large saucepan halfway with water. Bring to a boil over high heat, then reduce the heat to low so the water is barely simmering.

2. In a large bowl, beat the eggs, sugar, lemon zest, and salt with a whisk until pale yellow and thick.

Whisk in the flour in two additions. Slowly drizzle in the milk, whisking constantly.

3. Place the bowl over the pot of just-simmering water (taking care the bottom of the bowl is not touching the water) and whisk constantly for 5 to 7 minutes, until the mixture is thick and the taste of flour has subsided. After 3 to 4 minutes, switch to a spatula to smooth out any remaining lumps, though it's fine if just a few remain.

4. Transfer the mixture to a shallow bowl. Let it cool for 15 minutes. Cover it with a layer of plastic wrap directly touching the mixture to prevent a film from forming. Chill it in the fridge for at least 1 hour.

5. Place the crumbs in a wide, shallow vessel. Using a small scoop, melon baller, or teaspoon, scoop out the custard and drop balls—four or five at a time—into the crumbs. If the custard begins to stick to the scoop, dip it in hot water. Roll the balls to coat them with the crumbs, then transfer them to a large plate. Chill the balls, covered, in the freezer for at least 1 hour.

6. In a small, high-sided saucepan, heat the oil over medium heat to about 365°F. If you don't have a deep-fry thermometer, test the oil by dropping in a few bread crumbs; when the oil is hot enough, they should sizzle immediately and float. When the oil is heated, using a slotted spoon or spider, lower in four or five balls and cook them for about 1 minute, flipping them to ensure even browning, until lightly golden all over. Transfer the balls to a paper-towel-lined plate to drain. Repeat with the remaining custard balls.

7. Transfer the balls to a serving platter. Sift them with confectioners' sugar and serve immediately.

NO-BAKE
CHOCOLATE-COCONUT COOKIES

MAKES 24 (2-INCH) COOKIES

No-bake cookies are a boon for anyone in need of a no-fuss treat made entirely from pantry items. Many no-bake cookies call for peanut butter, which helps the batter hold its shape. But here, peanut butter has been replaced with dried bread crumbs, which not only provide a pleasant crunch but also make these nut-free and therefore safe for sharing with anyone. Be sure to plan ahead: while the batter takes no time to mix up, the shaped cookies must chill for at least 30 minutes before serving.

¾ cup unsweetened shredded coconut

1 cup sugar

½ cup (1 stick) unsalted butter

¼ cup 2 percent or whole milk

1½ tablespoons cocoa

1 teaspoon vanilla extract

1¼ cups Homemade Dried Bread Crumbs (page 178) or panko

1. In a small sauté pan, toast the coconut over medium heat until golden, about 5 minutes. Transfer to a plate to cool.

2. Meanwhile, in a medium saucepan, combine the sugar, butter, milk, cocoa, and vanilla over medium heat. Bring to a boil, then cook for 2 minutes, stirring constantly, adjusting the heat as needed to maintain a gentle boil.

3. Add the crumbs and toasted coconut to the saucepan and stir to combine. Portion the batter by tablespoonfuls onto a parchment-lined sheet pan. Gently flatten the cookies into 2-inch rounds.

4. Chill in the fridge for at least 30 minutes before serving. Store in an airtight container in the refrigerator for up to 1 week.

GOAT'S MILK GELATO
WITH SALTED CARAMEL CRUMBS

MAKES 1½ QUARTS GELATO; MAKES 1 CUP CRUMBS

The dessert chapter of *Italian Easy*, by Rose Gray and Ruth Rogers, is filled with simple ice creams and sorbets, many of which call for only three or four ingredients. Years ago, my mother and I fell in love with their mascarpone sorbet, made with mascarpone, lemon, sugar, and water, not only for its simplicity—no eggs makes mixing the base a total breeze—but also for its adaptability: the mascarpone is key, but the remaining ingredients can be used as a guide. In the summer, my mother combines it with puréed strawberries, lime zest, and sugar to taste, a treat that instantly endears her to her eight little grandchildren.

This tangy, goat's milk gelato, as well as the ones on pages 242 and 243, adhere to this formula, and each is showered with crunchy, caramelized crumbs—in essence, sweetened *pangrattato* (see page 166) that is delicious with fresh or roasted fruit and custardy desserts as well.

for the gelato

1½ cups mascarpone cheese

¾ cup sugar

1 cup goat's milk

for the crumbs

2 tablespoons (¼ stick) unsalted butter

1 cup fresh bread crumbs (see Note, page 172)

Pinch of sea salt

1 tablespoon sugar

Caramel (see page 156), for serving

Flaky sea salt, such as fleur de sel, for serving

1. Make the gelato: In the bowl of a stand mixer fitted with the paddle attachment, beat the mascarpone until light, about 30 seconds. Add the sugar and goat's milk and beat until smooth and the sugar is completely dissolved, about 1 minute more. Chill the mixture, covered, in the refrigerator for at least 1 hour.

2. Meanwhile, make the crumbs: In a large skillet, melt the butter over medium heat. Add the crumbs and the salt and stir frequently for about 5 minutes until the crumbs begin to turn light brown—the mixture may bubble or look foamy. Sprinkle in the sugar and cook until the crumbs are golden brown, 3 to 5 minutes more. Transfer the crumbs to a plate to cool. They will crisp further as they sit.

3. Churn the chilled goat's milk mixture according to your ice cream maker's instructions. Transfer the mixture to a storage container—a wide vessel such as a loaf pan makes for easy scooping. If the mixture is especially soft, freeze for at least 1 to 2 hours before serving.

4. To serve, scoop the gelato into bowls, scatter over the crumbs, drizzle with caramel, and sprinkle with a pinch of sea salt.

COFFEE GELATO
WITH COCOA CRUMBS

MAKES 1½ QUARTS GELATO; MAKES 2 CUPS CRUMBS

When tiny cubes of bread caramelize on the stovetop in butter and sugar and dive into a bowl of cocoa to cool, they become irresistibly crunchy. Coffee gelato so nicely complements these chocolaty crumbs, though it's hard to imagine a flavor that wouldn't welcome this garnish—strawberry, mint, peanut butter, vanilla. The cocoa crumbs can be made ahead and stored in an airtight container for at least a week.

for the gelato

¼ cup boiling water

1 tablespoon instant espresso

1½ cups mascarpone cheese

1 cup whole or 2 percent milk

¾ cup sugar

for the cocoa crumbs

1 tablespoon unsweetened cocoa, sifted if there are lumps

3 tablespoons unsalted butter

2 cups ¼-inch-cubed bread, such as peasant bread (see page 22), Soft Sandwich Bread (page 74), or Light Brioche (page 92), crusts removed

Pinch of sea salt

3 tablespoons sugar

1. Make the gelato: In a small bowl, pour the boiling water over the instant espresso. Stir to dissolve.

2. In the bowl of a stand mixer fitted with the paddle attachment, beat the mascarpone until light, about 30 seconds. Add the milk and sugar and beat until smooth and the sugar is completely dissolved, about 1 minute more. Add the ¼ cup espresso and beat to incorporate. Chill the mixture in the refrigerator for at least 2 hours.

3. Meanwhile, make the cocoa crumbs: Place the cocoa in a small bowl. In a small skillet, melt the butter over medium-high heat. When the foam subsides, reduce the heat to medium, add the cubed bread and a pinch of sea salt, and cook until lightly golden, about 5 minutes. Add the sugar and cook until lightly caramelized, 5 minutes more—it will feel like a lot of sugar, and the mixture in the pan will look liquidy. Scrape the bread into the bowl with cocoa and toss to coat. Spread the coated bread onto a plate to crisp, about 15 minutes. Once cool, transfer to a resealable plastic bag and crush lightly with a rolling pin until the crumbs are the size of peas.

4. Churn the gelato mixture according to your ice cream maker's instructions. Transfer the mixture to a storage container—a wide vessel such as a loaf pan makes for easy scooping. If the mixture is especially soft, freeze for at least 1 to 2 hours before serving.

5. To serve, sprinkle the cocoa crumbs over the coffee gelato, passing any extra crumbs on the side.

LIME GELATO
WITH TOASTED COCONUT CRUMBS

MAKES 1½ QUARTS GELATO; MAKES 1 CUP CRUMBS

Here, a healthy measure of lime zest punctuates the mascarpone-based gelato, subtly infusing it with citrus and floral notes, a refreshing foil for sugared, toasted coconut crumbs. Make the crumbs ahead and store in an airtight container at room temperature; they'll keep for up to a week.

for the gelato

1½ cups mascarpone cheese

1 cup whole or 2 percent milk

¾ cup sugar

Finely grated zest of 2 limes

for the crumbs

¼ cup unsweetened shredded coconut

2 teaspoons coconut oil

¼ cup Homemade Dried Bread Crumbs (page 178) or panko

2 teaspoons sugar

1. Make the gelato: In the bowl of a stand mixer fitted with the paddle attachment, beat the mascarpone until light, about 30 seconds. Add the milk and sugar and beat until smooth and the sugar is completely dissolved, about 1 minute more. Add the lime zest and beat to incorporate. Chill the mixture in the refrigerator for at least 2 hours.

2. Meanwhile, make the crumbs: In a small skillet, toast the coconut over medium heat until golden, about 5 minutes. Transfer to a plate. Add the oil, crumbs, and sugar to the same pan still set over medium heat. Cook until the crumbs are golden, about 4 minutes. Add the coconut back into the pan, stir to combine, then transfer the mixture to a plate to cool.

3. Churn the gelato mixture according to your ice cream maker's instructions, then transfer to a storage container—a wide vessel such as a loaf pan makes for easy scooping. Freeze for 1 to 2 hours before serving.

4. To serve, sprinkle the toasted coconut crumbs over the lime gelato, passing any extra crumbs on the side.

FAQ

Can I use active dry yeast?

If you do choose to use active dry yeast, here's how: In a small bowl, dissolve the sugar into the water. Sprinkle the yeast on top. Let it stand for 10 to 15 minutes or until the mixture is foamy; there is no need to stir it up. Meanwhile, in a large bowl, whisk together the flour and salt. When the yeast mixture is foamy, stir it up and add it to the flour. Using a rubber spatula, mix until the liquid is absorbed and the ingredients form a sticky dough ball. Proceed with each bread recipe as written.

To adapt any other recipes to active dry yeast, be sure the liquid ingredients are lukewarm. Dissolve the yeast into the lukewarm water with a teaspoon of the sweetener (whatever is being called for: sugar, honey, molasses, etc.). Let it stand for 10 to 15 minutes, or until the mixture is foamy; there is no need to stir it up. When the mixture is foamy, combine it with the dry ingredients, and proceed with the recipe as written.

Why doesn't my bread rise as high as the loaves in your photos?

The biggest culprit is the vessel. See Equipment (page 16) and Four Tips to Ensure Each Loaf Is a Success (page 27) for advice regarding baking equipment.

The second culprit is over-rising. The first rise should take 1 to 2 hours. For the second rise, let the dough rise only until it crowns the rim of the bowl or loaf pan—it will spring higher in the oven. If the dough begins spilling over the edges of the vessel during its second rise, deflate it with forks, and let it rise again.

Why do rising times vary so dramatically?

Many variables—humidity, water temperature, flour, yeast, environment—affect the dough you mix, and every day these factors change. In the summer, your dough may rise in 1 hour; in the winter, it may take as long as 2. Second rises, too, may take 10 minutes when it is warm out; they may take 25 minutes when it's cold. For the first rise, a slightly warm oven will help the dough rise nicely no matter the conditions outside (see Four Tips to Ensure Each Loaf Is a Success, page 27).

Why do you bake the bread initially at 425°F, then reduce the heat?

Starting the baking off at a higher temperature encourages the dough to spring in the oven. Lowering the temperature after 15 minutes ensures the loaves don't brown too quickly.

How should I store my bread? How should I reheat my bread?

See Preserving Bread (page 27).

Can you mix the dough at night and bake it in the morning? Or mix the dough in the morning before work?

Yes. See Make It Ahead (page 27).

Can you bring the dough to a party and bake it on the premises?

Yes. See Make It Ahead (page 27).

Is there a vegan substitute for butter for greasing the bowls?

Yes. See Butter (page 20).

Can I double the recipe? Halve it?

Yes. When doubling, however, 3 teaspoons of instant yeast will suffice. When halving, use 1 teaspoon instant yeast.

I find using forks tricky to lift the dough into the bowls. What else can I use?

Flexible bowl scrapers (also called dough scrapers or bench scrapers) work well for portioning and scooping dough. Otherwise, try to use wide forks with short tines.

How can I make this bread more artisan?

If you equate "artisan" with a thick, bronze, crackling crust, the easiest way to adapt the Peasant Bread Master Recipe (page 22) to this style is to keep the proportions the same but to bake the dough in a preheated vessel, the genius method Jim Lahey introduced (via Mark Bittman and the *New York Times*) to the home baker in 2006. To give the Peasant Bread the Lahey treatment, while the dough is making its first rise (in a warm spot, but not your oven), preheat a Dutch oven for 45 minutes at 450°F. Dust a clean surface with ¼ cup (32 g) flour. Turn the dough out onto the clean surface and shape the dough into a ball using the pinkie-edges of your hands to pinch the dough underneath, creating tension. Transfer the dough to a sheet of parchment paper—the use of parchment paper here is key, as it allows for a seamless transition from the counter to the preheated Dutch oven. After 20 minutes of resting on the counter, remove the Dutch oven from the oven, lower the Peasant Bread, parchment paper and all, into the pan, cover, and bake for 30 minutes. Uncover and bake for 15 minutes more.

If you equate "artisan" with a more porous crumb and a slight sour flavor, you can reduce the amount of yeast and extend the rise times. Simply use 1 teaspoon instant yeast and cold water in place of the boiling water. Let the dough rise overnight or for 10 to 12 hours at room temperature, then proceed with the recipe.

Alternatively, you can follow the recipe exactly, but let the dough rise in the fridge.

With either of these methods, the second rise may take as long as 1 to 2 hours.

If you equate "artisan" with using flour sourced from a local mill or flour milled at home, follow the Peasant Bread Master Recipe (page 22) exactly as written. You may have to adjust with more flour or water to achieve the desired consistency. See Troubleshooting (page 248).

Can I make bread without salt?
Yes, but the loaves will taste bland.

How can I give my loaves a shiny crust?
Make an egg wash: whisk 1 egg with 1 tablespoon of water. Brush this over the dough before baking.

How can I make dried bread crumbs if I don't have a food processor?

SLOW METHOD
Preheat the oven to 250°F. Tear the bread approximately into 1-inch pieces. Spread them on a sheet pan and toast for 45 to 60 minutes, until very dry; the crumbs should take on very little color. Cool them completely on the sheet pan. Transfer the pieces to a resealable plastic bag and crush with a rolling pin or bash with a skillet. Store in an airtight container at room temperature for months.

FAST METHOD
Preheat the oven to 375°F. Tear the bread approximately into 1-inch pieces. Spread them on a sheet pan and toast for 10 to 15 minutes, until evenly golden. Cool them completely on the sheet pan. Transfer the pieces to a resealable plastic bag and crush with a rolling pin or bash with a skillet. Store in an airtight container at room temperature for months.

Why do I need to dry the crumbs? Can't I just let them get stale?
Drying out the crumbs is preferable to staling because drying preserves the flavor. Antonietta Fazzone, a friend's mother (see page 217), demonstrated this to me one day at her sink, where she ran a slice of bread she had dried out in the oven under the streaming faucet. She then broke off a piece for me to taste. Then, she ran a slice of stale bread under the faucet. She handed me that piece to compare, but there was no comparison—the one she had oven-dried was the unmistakable winner. Toasting had preserved the flavor; staling had not.

TROUBLESHOOTING

My loaves have muffin tops.
Solution: Your dough has over-risen. Be sure your vessel is the requisite size. Next time, on the second rise, let the dough only crown the rims of the vessels before sticking it in the oven. If you get distracted and your dough has risen too high—that is, it is spreading over the sides of the bowl—then gently deflate the dough in the bowl and let it rise again.

My top crust is too dark.
Solution: Bake the bread on a lower rack or bake the loaves at a lower temperature: 375°F for 40 to 45 minutes.

My bottom crust is too dark.
Solution: Bake the bread on a higher rack.

My loaf is pale all around.
Solution: If the loaves look pale after the recommended baking time, simply bake them longer, checking every 3 to 5 minutes. If this problem persists, consider buying an oven thermometer, which costs just a few dollars and will let you know the accuracy of your oven.

My dough is pourable.
Solution: Add ¼ cup (32 g) more flour. Continue adding flour in this manner until the dough forms a sticky ball—remember, however, that the Peasant Bread dough is not stiff and tacky like kneaded bread dough. If you live in a humid climate, you may have better success reducing the liquid by 2 to 4 tablespoons. You will find, too, that as the seasons change, you may need more or less water.

My dough is stiff, and I cannot incorporate all of the flour.
Solution: Add water 1 tablespoon at a time, mixing until the dough forms a sticky dough ball and all of the flour is incorporated. Too much flour likely caused the dough to be stiff. If you are not using a scale to measure the flour, do this instead: use a fork to fluff up the flour in the bag, spoon the flour into your measuring cups, then level it off. This method will ensure each cup of flour measured will be on the lighter side.

My dough is rising, and I have to go out unexpectedly.
Solution: Deflate the dough, pulling it toward the middle of the bowl. Scrape down the sides of the bowl with a spatula. Cover the bowl with plastic wrap or a tea towel and put it in the fridge. When you return, place the bowl in a warm place to rise.

My dough isn't rising.
Solution: Be sure to use warm water and to let the dough rise in a warm place. See Four Tips to Ensure Each Loaf Is a Success (page 27).

My dough didn't rise at all.
Solution: Buy new yeast and be sure you are using instant yeast. If you use active dry yeast, you must activate it in warm water first (see page 246.)

My sweet breads are browning too quickly.
Solution: Next time, lower your oven temperature by 25 degrees and extend the baking time for 5 to 10 minutes. You can also lower the temperature during baking.

I can't stop eating my homemade bread.
Solution: Give it away! A dear friend's mother said it best: "People who don't bake think bread is a miracle, and people who do appreciate the effort and good mojo." You will be forever loved.

Thank you to: The readers of *Alexandra's Kitchen,* for so much support over the years, for e-mailing and commenting, and for encouraging and inspiring me with many thoughtful questions and suggestions. This book would not be possible without you.

My family: My husband, Ben Stafford, for his love, honesty, encouragement, and support, and for eating without protest every slice, heel, crust, crumb, and melba toast during the making of this book (except for that one night he asked for a salad).

My children, Ella, Graham, Wren, and Tig, for their hearts, minds, and spirits, for making me feel so lucky every day.

My mother, Liza Lowery, for teaching me how to cook, for dedicating so much time and energy to this project in the kitchen and out, for allowing me to share her treasured recipe with the world, and for teaching me the importance of good bread on the table, second only to good company around it.

My three parents, Liza and Chip Lowery and Bill Cobbett, for giving me the best childhood, for loving me always, for teaching me the importance of family. My sister and brother, Lindsey and Nick Cobbett, the best siblings in the world, for their ability to make me laugh harder than anyone.

My dearest auntie Marcy and unclie Wade Weathers, for the many and most cherished memories in Vermont, for always opening their house and welcoming my family, for so many delicious meals, for their love and affection.

My mother- and father-in-law, Carole and Richard Stafford, for so much generosity and kindness over the years, for relocating halfway across the country to be near my family, for giving so much love to Ella, Graham, Wren, and Tig, and for all of their efforts getting my children across the country for the *Bread Toast Crumbs* photo shoot.

Vicki Stafford, my California mother, for so many fun outings, movie nights, and delicious dinners commenced with high-octane Jerry Stafford martinis, and for helping me with Ella when I needed it most.

Antonietta Fazzone, for opening her kitchen to me, feeding me pizza with morning coffee, and for teaching me how to make *limoncello,* prosciutto, and *pancotto,* the most delicious meal in the world.

Ellen Yin, for making my time at Fork challenging, rewarding, and fun, for teaching me why I should care about fresh, local food, and for continuing to inspire me with all that she does. Thien Ngo, for the many lunches at Nam Phuong, dinners at Tai Lake, and fried-egg breakfast sandwiches with Chinese sausage. I think about my time in the Fork kitchen every day.

To my recipe testers: Sandy Gluck, for her expertise, thoroughness, and guidance, Meredith Kurtzman, for her baking skills and knowledge, and Betsy Loth, for so much thoughtful feedback on the breads. Many thanks, too, to Kathleen Mary for her dedication to the gluten-free loaf, to Dana Dantzler, for her many loaf pan (and other) experiments, and Rebecca Kasper, for her enthusiasm for the whole-wheat loaves and many other recipes. Thank you to Carolyn Connors, babysitter and recipe tester extraordinaire, as well as to Sandra Buchanan, Tina Tighe, Linda Lucca, Cathe Casey, Hana Omiya, Tom Duff, and Dan Solomon. Thank you, too, to Gena Hamshaw for sharing her vegan knowledge and inspiration.

My agent, Berta Treitl, for believing in me, encouraging me, and being such a steady and positive guide on this journey.

The incredible team at Clarkson Potter, most especially my editor, Amanda Englander, for her belief in and enthusiasm for this project from day one and for so much insightful editing along the way. Many thanks, too, to Stephanie Huntwork and Ian Dingman for their beautiful design sense, as well as to Anna Mintz, Jana Branson, Carly Gorga, Patricia Shaw, Philip Leung, Doris Cooper, and Aaron Wehner.

Everyone on set at the photo shoot, foremost Eva Kolenko, for not only her stunning photographs but also her musical sensibilities, shoe collection, dance moves, and ordering skills at the lunch hour. Jeffrey Larsen, for his patience, organization, dedication, and keen artistic vision. Natasha Kolenko, for her beautiful prop collection, Emily Stewart, for assisting Eva and everyone, and Amy Hatwig and Veronica Laramie, for all of their help in the kitchen. Many thanks to my brother, Nick, for chauffeuring my mother and me around Oakland for ten days and being the best company at every delicious meal.

Finally, many dear friends, family, and advocates whose encouragement along the way has meant more than anything: Bates Barley, Amy Koch, Stephanie Sherman, EB Kelly, Lauren Walters, Chandra Lombard, Darcy Levy, Katy Annuschat, Lisa Malitz (the best host in NYC), Phoebe Lapine, Kristina Matsch, the Ouska family, the Buth family, the Bennett family, Kathrin Schwesinger, the Lepharts, Martha Sutro, Holly Loth, Judith Fenlon, Gautam Parthasarathy, Masako Yamada, Teal Reeves, Rose Hitt, and Kim Mastrianni.

Note: Page references in *italics*
indicate photographs.

Library of Congress
Cataloging-in-Publication Data
Names: Stafford, Alexandra, author. |
Lowery, Liza, author. Title: Bread toast
crumbs / Alexandra Stafford with Liza
Lowery. Description: New York : Clarkson
Potter, [2017] | Includes index. Identifiers:
LCCN 2016022076| ISBN 9780553459838
(hardcover : alk. paper) | ISBN
9780553459845 (ebook) Subjects: LCSH:
Bread. | LCGFT: Cookbooks. Classification:
LCC TX769 .S7777 2017 | DDC 641.81/5—
dc23 LC record available at https://lccn.loc.
gov/2016022076.

ISBN 978-0-553-45983-8
Ebook ISBN 978-0-553-45984-5

Printed in China

Book and cover design by Ian Dingman
Cover photographs by Eva Kolenko

10 9 8 7 6 5 4 3 2 1

First Edition

"Alexandra's book makes you want to kick over everything and spend your days in the kitchen baking simple, no-knead loaves and turning them into the best parts of every meal. *Bread Toast Crumbs*. The title tells you everything except how creative, practical and delicious the recipes are."

—DORIE GREENSPAN

"From crusts to crumbs, from home-style, multigrain loaves to zippy shakshuka rounds, *Bread Toast Crumbs* presents a wide range of breads and is the perfect guide for bakers wanting to explore the world of possibilities for making their own loaves, and using every slice and crumb that doesn't get gobbled up right away."

—DAVID LEBOVITZ

"*Bread Toast Crumbs* is part useful expertise, part gentle advice, and all heart. This book is a new essential volume for the home bread-baker, and a great testament to the worth of taking something good and using it to its absolute fullest."

—ALANA CHERNILA

"I can't go a single day without bread, so what a treat it was to find this beautiful book celebrating one of my favorite foods to both make and eat. It's chockablock with approachable yet sophisticated recipes that deliver mouthwatering results, from Vinaigrette Toasts to meatloaf made with buttermilk-soaked bread and even breadcrumb-studded chocolate bark, a brilliant riff on the age-old snack of bread and chocolate."

—LUISA WEISS

"As someone who loves to bake bread, eat toast, and cook for my family and friends, I am excited about this book. It's approachable (no-knead!) and has gorgeous photos. Alexandra has so many clever ideas on how to take that bread a step further for dishes I'll make on weeknights or to entertain."

—ERIN GLEESON